MOLLY
ON THE
RANGE

MOLLY ON THE RANGE

recipes and stories
from an unlikely life on a farm

MOLLY YEH

creator of my name is yeh

RODALE.

RODALE *wellness*

Live happy. Be healthy. Get inspired.

Sign up today to get exclusive access to our authors, exclusive bonuses, and the most authoritative, useful, and cutting-edge information on health, wellness, fitness, and living your life to the fullest.

Visit us online at RodaleWellness.com
Join us at RodaleWellness.com/Join

Rodale books may be purchased for business or promotional use or for special sales. For information, please write to:
Special Markets Department, Rodale Inc., 733 Third Avenue, New York, NY 10017.

Printed in China

Rodale Inc. makes every effort to use acid-free ∞, recycled paper ♻.

Book design by Rae Ann Spitzenberger

Photographs by Chantell Quernemoen: ii–iii, xv, xvi, 12, 15, 36, 42, 49, 55, 56, 86, 88, 91, 106, 122, 131, 132, 138, 143, 154, 159 (left), 160 (top), 163, 188, 191, 192, 199, 202, 234, 268, 274, 284

All other photographs by Molly Yeh

Illustrations and lettering by Lisel Jane Ashlock

Library of Congress Cataloging-in-Publication Data is on file with the publisher.

ISBN-13: 978–1–62336–695–7

Distributed to the trade by Macmillan

2   4   6   8   10   9   7   5   3   hardcover

We inspire health, healing, happiness, and love in the world. Starting with you.

To my parents, my Eggparents, and Eggboy.

And to readers of my name is yeh.

CONTENTS

INTRODUCTION

Hi! My name is Molly. I live on a farm in the upper Midwest with my husband, the Internet, 12 hens named Macaroni, and a plump rooster named Tofu.

I'm originally from the suburbs of Chicago, where I led a childhood of hosting lemonade stands, writing in stacks of Hello Kitty diaries, and every so often pulling out all of my mom's pots and pans to play a drum solo with her spoons and whisks. My existence was fueled by Lunchables, Handi-Snacks, and macaroni and cheese—any food that was white, orange, or brown, and no food that wasn't.

There was always music around the house. My dad played the clarinet and my older sister, Stoopie, played the piano and violin. In fourth grade, I followed my love for hitting things, and enrolled in the school band as a percussionist. I fell so wildly in love with classical music that when I graduated high school, I moved to New York to study at Juilliard.

Manhattan is the most exciting place to live for a suburban teenage bean! Every night there were concerts to see, neighborhoods to explore, and new restaurants to try.

The city swallowed me whole, and the only way out was to try every slice of pizza and every fancy cheeseburger, and to make up for lost time spent on a picky childhood by seeking out obscure tasting menus and hidden izakayas.

In 2009, the diaries that I'd kept since childhood morphed into an online blog, because that was an easy way to pair photographs with my entries and then share them with my family and friends. I no longer had to pretend that aliens in the future digging up my notebooks from an underground safe were my only audience. With colorful fonts and saturated photos, I blogged about my everyday life, little adventures around the city, and all of the new food that I was having so much fun trying.

After graduating from Juilliard, I moved out to Brooklyn and spent my days writing, playing music gigs around the city, working part time at Juilliard's newspaper, and in my off time, eating and blogging for fun. I had a kitchen that was sunny and spacious (for New York) and I never wanted to leave. More and more my blog started filling up with recipes and styled food photos.

Around that time, I reconnected with an old college classmate: a slightly older trombonist who had spent a few post-graduation

years on his family's farm on the North Dakota–Minnesota border but had just moved back to the city to play music. His name is Nick, but eventually he earned the nickname Eggboy (see page 14), and we fell in wuv.

Together we discovered our fierce inner homebodies and began spending our weekends inside or playing catch in the park. We were the worst New Yorkers ever. We missed the Midwest and wanted to be closer to our families, so after a lot of thinking and thinking, we packed up all of our things and moved west to Grand Forks, North Dakota.

Fearing that I would go into shock over the drastic change between city and farm, Eggboy and I got an apartment in downtown Grand Forks, which is like Stars Hollow

but way colder, like –30°F. Eggboy went to work farming sugar beets and wheat with his pop, I got a job at the town bakery, and since I didn't have any friends for my first few months of living here, my free time was spent working on my blog and growing a following beyond my mom and Eggmom.

Eventually, through working on my photos and recipes and using websites like Pinterest to drive traffic to my site, I started picking up work developing blog posts for other sites and partnering with brands to create content for my site, and blogging became my full-time job—which was exciting because working from home and never having to shower is one thing I really like to do.

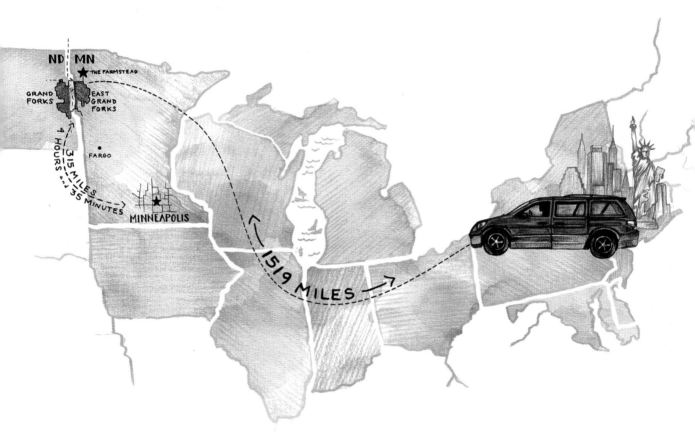

ND | MN

★ THE FARMSTEAD

GRAND
FORKS

EAST
GRAND
FORKS

4 HOURS and 35 MINUTES

315 MILES

• FARGO

MINNEAPOLIS
★

1519 MILES

Beyond the blog, my adjustment to the upper Midwest had its great moments and its interesting moments. I fell in love with Grand Forks, its quality of life, and all of the storms that snowed us in, but got confused over some of the new foods here like hotdish, Jell-O salad, and cookie salad.

Over time I warmed up to them and improved my Tater Tot casserole skills (page 146). I got the hang of lefse (see page 207) and found an appreciation for local specialties like rhubarb and venison. I also began re-creating all of the foods that I missed from back in New York but couldn't get in Grand Forks, like falafel and fresh pita, and steamed buns and knishes.

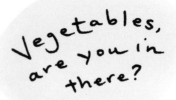

After about a year spent in downtown Grand Forks, Eggboy and I moved out to the house on his family's farmstead, where his grandparents had lived for the decades before that, and where his great-great-grandpa Bernt had settled after coming over from Norway in 1876. The farmstead is just a few miles outside of town, right over the border, in Minnesota. Out our back door, farmland goes on to the horizon, but out the front door, emergency mayonnaise is just a 5-minute drive away.

This is my home, it's where I spend my days baking, blogging, and tending to the chickens, and my nights cooking supper for Eggboy and relishing all that is this rural way of life.

If you had told me in college that in 5 years I'd be living on a farm in the upper Midwest, I would have shoved my bodega sandwich in your face.

A NOTE ON THE RECIPES

Contrary to what growing up in Illinois might suggest, nothing truly prepared me for the vegetable-less salads and big creamy casseroles that I met when I moved to Grand Forks, but this town is basically the North Pole so I don't know how I was expecting anything other than creamed soups and limited access to fresh vegetables. This was all slightly jarring, but I quickly found that digging into my mother-in-law's church cookbooks, re-creating these dishes, and tweaking them to fit my tastes was my favorite way of getting to know my new community. And likewise, I love introducing my new neighbors to the food of my people, and using from-scratch recipes to keep the traditions that I grew up with alive and well in this little challahless, babkaless town.

Just like the recipes on my blog, the recipes in this book are representative of my Jewish and Chinese heritage, my time spent in New York and traveling abroad to Israel and Europe, my '90s suburban upbringing, and my new upper Midwest surroundings. There are a lot of everyday recipes in here as well as some things you should make when you have an entire free weekend or a special occasion coming up. Most of them require common grocery store ingredients (because chances are if I can find it in my town, you can find it in yours), but if you need to sub out one vegetable for another or if you'd like to use your fancy obscure cheese instead of whatever's listed, go right ahead. These recipes are meant to be fun and enjoyable!

NOTES ON INGREDIENTS

Flour: Unless otherwise specified, any time flour is called for, that means unbleached all-purpose flour. One of the best things that I learned from Martha Stewart was that it's okay to never want to sift. The fluff and scoop method, of fluffing up the flour with a scoop to aerate it and then carefully scooping up the fluffed stuff and leveling it, is perfectly okay, and it's how I usually measure flour.

FLOUR AND BREAD
When kneading bread, the most important thing that you can do is not add too much flour. Only add it when its stickiness becomes a hindrance, and stop the moment that it isn't. Too much flour will make your bread dry.

Olive oil: For a long time I mega rolled my eyes at people who listed their Number One Kitchen Must-Have as "really good olive oil." I did not get the act of cooking eggs in fancy expensive olive oil when you just salt and hot sauce the shit out of them anyway, and I was afraid of even using it that often for fear of its low smoke point. But then two things happened: The head of the olive department at UC Davis looked me in the eye and said that good olive oil has a smoke point range of between 390°F and 400°F (meaning you can even deep-fry in it) and then I did a side-by-side blind tasting of high-quality extra virgin olive oil versus a cheaper low-quality one and the low-quality one tasted like peepee. So now I pay attention to the quality of my olive oils and typically turn to California Olive Ranch's because it tastes good and you can deep-fry with it.

Flavorless oil: A lot of my recipes call for flavorless oil, which can refer to canola oil, vegetable oil, or any oil that has a neutral flavor and, in most cases, a high smoke point. My rule of thumb is that I'll use olive oil if I'm cooking in a pan with a small coating of oil (as opposed to, say, ½ or 1 inch of oil) only if the stove temperature doesn't go above medium or if I plan on keeping a close eye on it to make sure it doesn't start smoking. For anything above medium heat, I usually use canola. In cakes, I typically use canola as well, but coconut oil is a great option, too.

Butter: Salted butter is for spreading on fresh hot bread, unsalted butter is for everything else. In an ideal world, we all have endless amounts of good grass-fed butter that comes in blocks or rolls, not sticks, and the cows who make it all have cow names like Bessie and Fran. But that can get expensive, so I'll just encourage this simple guideline: In a recipe where the buttery flavor is going to shine through, such as in a buttercream frosting, polenta, or any fresh bread that you're going to be slathering with butter as soon as it comes out of the oven, grass-fed butter is worth sacrificing the fancy latte drink or whatever you were going to spend that extra $3 on. In a cookie dough or cake, there's usually enough other stuff mixed in that no one's going to get that offended if you use less expensive, non-grass-fed generic butter.

Salt: I keep a jar of Morton's kosher salt next to my stove and that's what I use for just about everything, except for when I want to get fancy and finish a dish with Maldon flaky sea salt or smoked flaky sea salt. Salting is the most important part of cooking because it makes the flavors the best they can be. So if you don't do it already, learn to salt every layer of your dish, not just at the end.

Pie dough: Listen. I'm not a Sarah Kieffer. I'm not a Yossy Arefi. I am a moderate member of #TeamCake and I don't have a family pie crust tradition. Maybe it's that my

fine motor skills are discouraged by the beautiful piecrust designs on Instagram or maybe I'm a little scared by the passionate shortening vs. butter and water vs. vodka arguments that I've witnessed with my own two eyes or maybe it's that so much fear has been instilled in me w/r/t not overmixing the dough or else it will get tough, but I have never felt compelled to dirty up my food processor in the name of homemade piecrust and therefore always use store-bought. *Exhales* I'm no phony, I tried my fair share of homemade crusts until it no longer brought me joy, so I Kondo-punted it out of my life and have never looked back.

Pizza dough: Jim Lahey's no-knead pizza dough saved me. It cured the small amount of bitterness I fostered on Friday nights when we first moved here when I would have to face the fact that New York pizza was two flights away. Every Thursday night, a reminder goes off on my phone to start my pizza dough for the next night. I weigh my ingredients (buying a kitchen scale is worth it for this alone), mix mix mix, and put my dough to bed to rest up for its big event. Most of the pizza recipes in the book were developed with Jim's dough on a baking steel, but I also love Amy Thielen's cracker crust pizza from *The New Midwestern Table*, and I'm also not opposed to the occasional store-bought crust.

Marzipan: Marzipan is one of my most favorite things on the planet. I keep a steady supply of it on hand for all kinds of different uses in desserts and as decorations. It's an easy and fun way to decorate desserts and it tastes way better than fondant. I stock up whenever I go to Europe because I find that the quality and malleability of their store-bought marzipan is better than that in the States. Of course, making it from scratch is the ideal way to go (page 247), especially if you're serving it on its own or dipped in chocolate, but buying store-bought to use in baked goods or as a decoration is perfectly okay. Marzipan is usually found in the baking aisle and it's most commonly sold in either 7-ounce or 8-ounce packages (or you may luck out and find the 11-ounce can). In most of the recipes here where marzipan is required (Dark Chocolate Marzipan Scone Loaf on page 48, or Marzipan and Sea Salt Mandel Bread on page 219), that 1 ounce of marzipan won't make a big enough difference that would warrant you buying an entire extra 7-ounce package to make 8 ounces, hence the 7- to 8-ounce ingredient measurement in these.

Eggs: All measurements and timings in this book are written for large eggs. However, if you're working with eggs of a different size for a nonbaking recipe, simply adjust the suggested cooking times up or down depending on the egg size. If you're adjusting for a baking recipe, get out your scale and use 56 to 63 grams of egg for every egg called for in the recipe. My beliefs about egg quality are similar to that of butter. In a perfect world we all have a flock of chickens or at least a generous chicken-owning friend to deliver flavorful eggies with bright orange yolks that come from happy chickens who can forage all day and cuddle all night. If that's not the case, using any old eggs when making breads and cakes and anything where the egg flavor isn't front and center is just fine. But for egg-centric dishes like *shakshuka*, hole in the middles, and Scotch eggs, splurging on local happy eggs is 100 percent worth it.

Tahini: With a peanut allergic mom, I grew up with tahini in the place of peanut butter in a lot of recipes, and I always viewed it as peanut butter's fancy older sibling. It's so good in everything! Sweets, sauces, dressings, and of course hummus. . . . My dream house has tahini on tap, coming right out of a direct pipeline from the Middle East because that's where all the best tahini is. Stocking up on Al Arz, Karawan, or Har Bracha brands is worth checking an additional suitcase for if you go to Israel (you can also find them at some Middle Eastern stores in New York or if you hunt around online). They're so smooth and pure tasting. Stateside, Whole Foods 365, Seed + Mill, and Soom are my choices, but Joyva will also do in a pinch.

Coconut milk: Between writing kosher recipes for the *Jewish Daily Forward*, catering to a sometimes-dairy-free husband and his vaguely vegan family, and wanting to update and healthify the creamed soup component of just about every midwestern recipe I come across, I go through an ass-ton of coconut milk. My local grocery store has about six different brands in six different aisles at six different prices; it's the weirdest. The only tip I have when shopping for coconut milk is to buy the stuff that only contains coconut and water and maybe guar gum. Some coconut milks contain a ton of additives that taste and smell icky. Don't go there.

Yogurt: I always keep a large tub of plain, full-fat yogurt on hand for use in both sweet and savory recipes. Greek strained yogurt is my favorite (or sometimes I use Icelandic skyr) and oftentimes I go the extra mile and strain them even further in a cheesecloth to make Labneh (page 38). Greek yogurt and labneh are usually interchangeable, except for in cases where avoiding the extra whey makes a noticeable difference. In these cases I've specifically listed only labneh in the ingredients.

Nuts: I typically buy nuts in bulk, either raw or roasted, and always unsalted if possible. Salted nuts can tend to be too salty for some recipes, but if that's what you've got, remove the added salt from the recipe and use your best judgment to salt to taste. I typically toast my nuts in a cast iron pan over medium or medium-high heat until they're browned.

Broth bases: I love broth bases, both for making canned creamed soup substitutes and as seasonings on their own. My love is also for their convenience, a virtue I discovered when traveling home from the store when I lived in New York: Instead of lugging home cartons of broth, I could just get a handy jar of concentrated mix and then make my own at home. The brands I typically use are Orrington Farms and Better Than Bouillon, which both make chicken, beef, and vegetable bases.

Frozen vegetables: I use them! And you would too if you saw the fresh vegetables we get up here in the winter. Oh, for shame. It's hard, but having a stack of spinach blocks that will never wilt no matter how cold it is outside is so convenient, and it makes me appreciate our summer vegetables even more. One day I'll have a greenhouse up here, though, so we can have fresh vegetables all year round.

Tomatoes: Eggboy is in charge of our garden and he's really good at planting one seed of every variety of tomato that he can find. We get beefsteak tomatoes, Roma tomatoes, grape tomatoes. They're all good when they're fresh off the vine and still warm from the summer sun. Soon I will learn the ways of Eggmom, who is a champion at preserving summer tomatoes and freezing them for use in sauces and soups throughout the winter, but until then I'll be stocking up on tomatoes in the carton, from Pomi. I prefer those to cans because using the can opener is annoying and I read something on the Internet that said canned tomatoes will kill you. And even though I've never confirmed that, I'm still scared.

I

BREAKFAST
AND BRUNCH

THE SUBURBS

Everything about 4-year-old me was round: my belly, thanks to a hobby of hollowing out entire loaves of Wonder Bread in one sitting; my plump spherical tongue that stuck out perpetually (which somehow led to not one, but two diagnoses of mental retardation); and on top of my head the most fantastic and embarrassing bowl cut that took advantage of my Asianness to always hold its shape as perfectly as a Lego person, no matter how many trees I fell out of.

I grew up on a quiet old street in Glenview, Illinois, a northern suburb of Chicago, with my chocolatier-turned-homemaker-turned-school-social-worker mom, clarinetist dad, and older sister, whose name is Jenna, but for as long as I can remember we have called each other "Stoopie," which is possibly short for "stupid," but neither of us can remember. We had a rotating selection of goldfish, a couple of Westies named Polly and Phydo, and because I was a textbook kid of the '90s in suburban America, a Furby and a gaggle of Tamagotchis.

I went to public school and played AYSO soccer. My childhood smelled of normalcy and Fruit by the Foot.

During our summers, Stoopie and I regularly walked down the street to our neighbor Emily's house, where we would pee in her pool, sneeze about her pet bunny, and eat many many Town House crackers. Our evenings were spent with my mom on the lawn of Ravinia, where my dad played his concerts with the Chicago Symphony. On

a good night, I would demolish a baloney Lunchable and chocolate ice cream from the carousel-shaped parlor long before the trumpet calls from Beethoven's Leonore Overtures played over the loudspeaker to signify that the concert was about to start. On a mediocre night, everything would be the same, except my Lunchable would be turkey. At intermission, I changed into footie pajamas, and the chances were slim that I would still be awake for the final movement.

When my dad got time off from the orchestra, he and my mom and Stoop and I would pile into our white station wagon to vacation at Lake Lawn Resort in Lake Delavan, Wisconsin. Our resort of choice was a rustic sprawling lodge that had a very large great room, perfect for somersaults, and the snappiest breakfast buffet sausages that were perfect for sopping up syrup. Our drive there always required a stop in Richmond, Illinois, at Anderson's Candy Shop, a creaky Victorian house that sold nuggets of nougat, marzipan, and caramel dipped in thick layers of chocolate. Each one came in its own wax paper bag, blue letters for dark chocolate, red letters for milk. Dark chocolate–covered marzipan was Stoop's bar of choice; milk chocolate–covered marzipan was mine. And we would savor the life out of those things, taking little bite after little bite, making them last until they became gross and soggy.

When we tired of the horses, mini golf, swimming pools, and lake activities at our resort, our parents drove us down some very dusty gravel roads to Dam Road Bears, which sat in the middle of cornfields. Dam Road Bears was a crowded, warm house filled with stuffed animals and real animals, and you could make your own teddy bear. This was at least five years before Build-A-Bear surfaced, and it was way more advanced. It required building joints for your bears, which were structured and pastel colored, and sewing each one by hand to seal in the stuffing that you'd just spent a while fluffing. Each step was demonstrated by a calm old woman who lived cozily in her house of teddy bears. As someone who regularly took Amy the Teddy Bear to preschool, it was a magical little place.

The space between Lake Lawn Lodge and Dam Road Bears was the first real farmland I'd ever met. It was so flat and peaceful. The handful of houses we'd pass on the drive were classic white farmhouses that were, in my imagination, furnished with antique skillets and rocking chairs for their plump owners who all probably wore overalls and woke up before the sun. They'd have chickens who crowed at sunrise and one or two cows to milk. Maybe they had electricity, or maybe they didn't and just read by candlelight at night and used a weathervane for whatever weathervanes actually do. This is what I formulated in my mind from the back seat of the car with my new teddy bear. That's where the image associated with "farm" in my head was created, on a weekend getaway from the suburbs.

It was helpful because at school we'd often discuss the three places where one could live: a city, a suburb, a farm. City kids, in my mind, had slightly frizzy hair and moms who wore fashionably aggressive eye glasses; farm kids were all homeschooled and wore knitted sweaters. The world, I thought, revolved around my strip mall–covered suburb of Glenview, where all of my friends lived in two-story houses and had names that ended with an "ee" sound, Gracie, Lindsey, Gigi, and who shopped at Limited Too and wore flared denim and body glitter.

I was equally close-minded about my eating preferences. For the first 11 or 12 years of my life, the only foods that made it into my belly were white, orange, or brown. (Cheese, bread, matzo balls, etc.)

Miraculously, my mom took to this with grace. She mastered the hole-in-the-middle, which I'd eat twice daily in the name of protein, tapped Martha Stewart for the best ever homemade mac and cheese, and drove two towns over to Fresh Fields, before it became a Whole Foods, for nitrite-free Applegate baloney. She even read *D.W. the Picky Eater* to me every single night because it was my favorite book. If my pickiness freaked her out, she hid it from me well. Eventually she discovered that I'd eat carrots (they were orange, just like cheese!) and started requiring that I eat some before my after-dinner sundae cup. But really, she never forced me to eat when I wasn't hungry, and when I was hungry, I would eat. Even if it meant three Fuddruckers grilled cheeses right in a row during the major growth spurt of 2001. I was down with that. While my diet might not have been the healthiest at times, my mom saw a bigger picture that resulted in me having an excited relationship with food. The fact that she never forced me to eat things like broccoli meant that when I finally really came around to it (during college, at the No. 7 Sub in Manhattan, where a broccoli sandwich changes lives), I could approach it with a clean, excitable slate, free of any haunting childhood memories. Or when Brussels sprouts had their big moment, I could order the Má Pêche ones with glee without flashing back to not being able to leave the dinner table without finishing them.

The point is, everything my mom did went against what some Fancy Experts say about how you should force a food on a kid so many times until they eventually develop a taste for it. And alright, maybe that might have resulted in me liking green vegetables a few years earlier, but her way was awesome and brought about the enjoyment of some of the greatest ever snacks in the history of snacks, like bread and butter "sushi," Wonder Bread bread balls, and the embarrassing yet delightful Hot Dog Cheese.

HOT DOG CHEESE

Makes 1 serving

This is the first recipe I ever mastered. It was taught to me by my childhood neighbor Stephanie, probably during a *Baby-Sitters Club*–themed slumber party. It spurred a years-long obsession with hot dogs, which included an Oscar Mayer–themed birthday party and a failed audition at an open casting call for the Oscar Mayer commercial.

1 precooked hot dog, cut into ½-inch pieces   Ketchup, for serving
1 slice American cheese, ripped into
½-inch pieces

Put the hot dog slices on a plate. Top them with the cheese pieces. Microwave until warm and the cheese is melted. Eat with ketchup. Celebrate your 6th birthday.

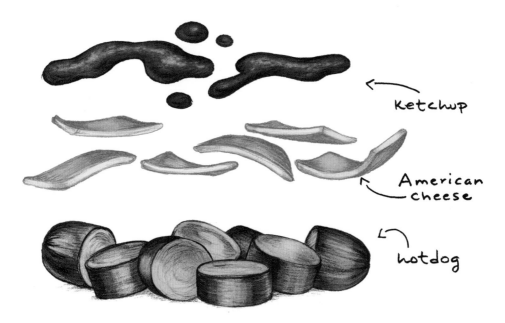

Ketchup

American cheese

hotdog

THE IDEAL HOLE IN THE MIDDLE

Makes 1 serving

You know those macho men who act all tough and they're like "I'm not gonna fight you, I'm not gonna fight you, I'm betta than that," blah blah, and then you say one thing about their mother and they sock you in the face? That's how I feel about the hole in the middle (or eggs in a basket, or toad in the hole, or if you're frisky, a one-eyed jack). Insult my omelet game or my bacon game, but don't go near my hole in the middle because just like Judy's hot chocolate in *The Santa Clause*, I've been perfecting it for 1,200 years.

Starting from when I was 8, I'd watch my mom make two of these suckers every single morning. Together at the breakfast table, we'd informally analyze them. "Is the yolk too firm?" "No." "Is it too runny?" "Maybe." "I'll put it back on the stove. What happened, did I flip it too soon?" "Nah." "Oy, the yolk didn't break, did it?" And so on and so forth. Ninety percent of the time they were perfect, with a firm white, a runny yolk, toasty bread, and coarse granules of salt sprinkled on at the end. And over time I've learned to be particular about a few things in order to increase the likelihood of perfection: I crack the egg into a bowl before pouring it into the pan to make sure the yolk doesn't break on the way out of the shell, and once the egg is in the hole, I *don't* flip it. I simply cover the pan and cook. A broken yolk is very bad news, y'all.

Unsalted butter or oil
1 slice of bread
1 large egg

Kosher salt and black pepper
Additional toppings, as desired (I like Tabasco sauce and a sprinkling of za'atar and sumac or a smashed avocado.)

In a large skillet, heat a thin layer of butter or oil over medium heat. Cut a round out of the bread using a biscuit cutter or a glass: A thinner 1/2-inch slice of bread will need about a 2- to 2 1/2-inch round; a thicker slice, like 1 1/2 inches, will need closer to a 1 1/2-inch round. Place both pieces in the skillet.

When the bread is lightly toasted on the bottom, turn it over, add a tiny bit more butter or oil to the middle of the hole if the pan is dry, and then add the egg. If you're dealing with a thick slice of bread, reduce the heat to low. If your slice is thinner than that, keep it on medium.

Cover the pan and cook until the white part of the egg is firm but the yolk is still runny. Check it often to avoid overcooking the yolk or use a glass lid so that you can keep an eye on the egg. Remove it from the heat, salt it ferociously, add a few turns of pepper and any desired toppings, and enjoy.

EVERYTHING BAGEL BOUREKAS WITH EGGS, SCALLIONS, AND CHEESE

Makes 6 servings

Every year my birthday begins with a breakfast sandwich and ends with fries (page 170). They're my two guiltiest pleasures, and I allow myself that one day a year to indulge in them shamelessly, pig-in-mud style. The breakfast sandwich doesn't have to be fancy; in fact it's the birthdays when I've woken up early enough to get to McDonald's in time for their breakfast (pre-2015 problems, amiright?) that have been up there on the list of tastiest birthday breakfasts. I like a fluffy egg, lots of cheese, maybe some sausage, and a croissant. Ooh I love it on a croissant. Or a bagel. And ketchup and hot sauce. And presents!

Anyway, we don't have bagels in Grand Forks, like, *at all*. There was a rumor floating around that in the early 2000s there was a bagel place in town that had bagels flown in every day from New York. Can you imagine?! It probably felt like that fake Prada store outside of Marfa. Only real. But I get by in the absence of bagels—knowing that I'll appreciate them so much more when I visit New York—by letting puff pastry sprinkled with everything bagel topping kind of fill this void.

So here's my puff-pastry ode to the breakfast sandwich, and we're going to call it a *boureka* because you feel a lot less guilty filling puff pastry with your favorite breakfast sandwich fillings if you call it a boureka and reminisce on your fun times in Israel as you eat it. Bourekas are a common snack throughout the Middle East and they're traditionally filled with cheese, potatoes, or meat. This one is a variation on the cheese type that takes a nod from the bagel in the form of scallion cream cheese and "everything bagel" topping, and plays the role of breakfast sandwich courtesy of a pile of fluffy cheesy scrambled eggs. These reheat well in the toaster, so go ahead and make a big batch so that you can have leftovers tomorrow for breakfast.

5 large eggs

2 tablespoons chopped chives

4 ounces shredded whole-milk mozzarella cheese

1 tablespoon unsalted butter

Kosher salt and black pepper

Tabasco sauce

1 sheet puff pastry, thawed in the refrigerator overnight

6 ounces scallion cream cheese, at room temperature (or 6 ounces plain cream cheese mixed with 2 scallions, finely chopped)

Everything Bagel Topping (recipe follows)

Ketchup, for serving

(recipe continues)

Preheat the oven to 375°F. Line a baking sheet with parchment paper.

In a medium bowl, whisk together 4 eggs until homogenous, then stir in the chives and mozzarella.

In a large skillet, heat the butter over medium heat. Pour the egg mixture into the hot skillet and cook until the bottom is set. Use a spatula to gently pull the bottom cooked parts to the sides of the pan to make space for more of the mixture to cook. Repeat this gentle pulling process one or two more times until a majority of the mixture is set and then transfer them to a bowl. The eggs should still be quite wet, as they'll continue to cook in the oven. Season them with salt and pepper and a few shakes of Tabasco sauce.

On a work surface, roll out the puff pastry to a 10 x 15-inch rectangle. Cut it into six 5-inch squares. Top each of the squares with a schmear of scallion cream cheese and a spoonful of the scrambled eggs, distributing them evenly and leaving a ¾-inch border around the edges.

In a small bowl, beat the remaining egg with 1 tablespoon water to make an egg wash. Brush the edges of the puff pastry squares with the egg wash, fold them in half, and pinch the edges to seal them well. Transfer them to the baking sheet, placing them 1 inch apart. Brush the tops with egg wash and top with the everything bagel topping. Bake until golden brown. Begin checking for doneness at 30 minutes. Let cool slightly and serve with ketchup.

Leftovers can be refrigerated and reheated in a toaster oven.

Everything Bagel Topping

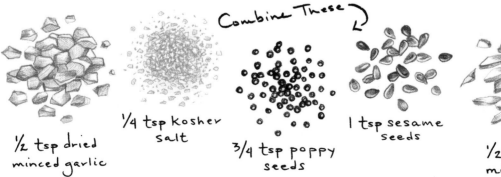

Combine These

½ tsp dried minced garlic

¼ tsp kosher salt

¾ tsp poppy seeds

1 tsp sesame seeds

½ tsp dried minced onion

PIGS IN A BLANKET ON A STICK

Makes 18 (9 servings)

From the time I was 8 years old until right before high school, when I decided to devote my waking hours to percussion, I spent all of my extracurricular activity units at the Glenview ice skating rink, attempting axels and doing twizzles. There were a ton of mornings that required team practices *before* school, before the sun rose, at like 5 a.m. I'd straight-up sleep in my tights the night before so that I wouldn't have to wrestle with them in the morning. Waking up that early was not cool, but it did often include the iconic pancake and sausage on a stick, the ultimate convenience breakfast.

Here's a big batch that you can make, freeze, and nuke for early mornings at the ice rink or wherever you're going.

2 tablespoons flavorless oil, plus more for deep-frying

1 cup flour

2 tablespoons sugar

¾ teaspoon kosher salt

½ teaspoon baking soda

1½ teaspoons baking powder

1 large egg

1 teaspoon vanilla extract

⅔ cup buttermilk

18 precooked breakfast sausages, thawed if frozen

18 wooden pop sticks or lollipop sticks

Maple syrup, optional, for serving

Pour 1½ inches of oil into a large heavy pot or high-sided skillet. Clip on a deep-fry thermometer and heat the oil over medium-high heat to 360°F.

In a medium bowl, whisk together the flour, sugar, salt, baking soda, and baking powder. In a separate small bowl or measuring cup, whisk together the egg, vanilla, 2 tablespoons oil, and buttermilk. Add the wet ingredients to the dry ingredients and stir to combine. Transfer the batter to a tall skinny glass or measuring cup (this step isn't completely necessary, but it will make coating the sausages easier). Working in batches of 3 or 4 sausages at a time, insert pop sticks or lollipop sticks into the sausages, pat off any excess moisture with a paper towel, and dip them into the pancake batter to fully coat. Carefully lower the entire thing (stick included) into the hot oil and fry until golden, about 2 minutes. Use tongs to transfer to a paper towel. Repeat with the remaining sausages. Cool slightly. Serve with maple syrup, if using.

Leftovers should be cooled completely, stored in an airtight container or zip-top bag in the freezer, and reheated in the microwave.

MUM'S MATZO BREI

Makes 4 servings

Your mom makes the best matzo brei! Your mom makes the best matzo brei! EVERYBODY'S MOM MAKES THE BEST MATZO BREI! Even if your mom puts cinnamon sugar all up in there (oof, I can't do that). Just for fun, and because I have so many eggs right now that my refrigerator is going to explode, and because my mom's matzo brei is excellent, shallot-y, and very hot sauce-y, here it is! If you've never had matzo brei, you should try it any time you want more out of your scrambled eggs in the way of texture, because it's not the flavor of the matzo that makes matzo brei good (there's no flavor in matzo anyway), it's the chewy texture of soaked matzo that's more al dente noodle than soggy cracker.

This is a popular dish for any meal during Passover, but I'd be lying if I told you that during the rest of the year I've never subbed out matzo for stale pita chips or saltines or Flamin' Hot Funyuns. And my mom would never do this, but if I'm ever feeling extra indulgent, I stir a tablespoon or two of heavy cream in with the eggs.

4 sheets matzo, roughly broken into 1-inch pieces

4 large eggs

2 tablespoons olive oil or butter

1 large shallot, finely chopped

Kosher salt and black pepper

Tabasco sauce, for serving

Fill a medium bowl with cold water and submerge the matzo. Soak for 1 minute, then drain.

In a separate medium bowl, whisk together the eggs until homogenous. Stir in the matzo and set aside.

In a large skillet, heat the oil or butter over medium heat. Add the shallot and a pinch of salt and cook, stirring occasionally, until soft and translucent, about 5 minutes.

Pour in the egg mixture and cook until the bottom is set. Use a spatula to gently pull the bottom cooked parts to the sides of the pan to make space for more of the mixture to cook. Repeat this gentle pulling process one or two more times until a majority of the mixture is set and then remove from the heat. The eggs should still be quite wet, but they'll continue to cook a bit in the pan. Continue folding them gently, and once they've reached your desired firmness, remove them from the pan and serve immediately. Season with salt and pepper and top with Tabasco.

EGGBOY

It started with Zac Efron, Zac Efron's abs, and a cholesterolly-free-spirited dietician who allowed it to go on record in an issue of *Men's Health* that, in order for Zac Efron to achieve his big bulky body for *The Lucky One*, he should probably eat one dozen eggs every single day. It was a factoid that the human futurely known as Eggboy took very very seriously, and it resulted in a diet that consisted almost exclusively of eggs, peanut butter, and spinach.

I had first met him (his real name is Nick) 5 years prior to the beginning of this diet, at Juilliard. He was an older, quiet, serious trombonist; I was a young, hungover percussionist. And the only real conversation we ever had while we were students was a respectable and in-depth debate in the cafeteria over the difference between "skinny fat" and "fat skinny," and other terms that followed a similar format, such as "creepy funny" versus "funny creepy."

For example: "Creepy funny," to me, is a humor that I would absolutely not want to be trapped alone in a small room with, while "funny creepy" is more harmless than that, like when you put pantyhose over face to look like Voldemort but underneath it's still you and you're not creepy. Nick believed it was the other way around and ultimately we agreed to disagree while alienating everyone at our lunch table.

Past that, our interactions were limited to performing Mahler 5 at Carnegie Hall together—where I was more concerned with the clarity of my bass drum licks and the location of the after party than the goings on in the trombone section—and salutations near the third-floor lockers. When you consider that nearly everybody you pass in the Juilliard hallways is either mentally preparing for their next rehearsal, emotionally recovering from their last lesson, too fixated on their posture to shift their gaze to you,

or Jon Batiste playing the melodica, a very basic and innocent "Hey Molly" goes an unnaturally long way.

So I had always considered Nick an honest, grounded, gentle human being, but we kept our distance partly because my friends and I were basically the opposite of all of that and I had a thing for meaty, douchey party boys with good text-messaging game. When Nick graduated, two years ahead of me, he fled the city to work on his family's farm and no one heard from him for a while.

And then 3 years later, on the eve of a breakup that would have me swearing off boys completely, he walked into a Sunday-night string quartet party way up at the top of Manhattan with my best friend Rob. He was wearing a T-shirt that exposed a fresh squiggly tattoo with jagged spikes coming out of it. It was a sugar beet, he explained. *It gets turned into sugar and we grow them on my family's farm. And oh yeah, I moved back to the city!*

Sugar beet

I was glad because Rob seemed so excited, but I was generally unaffected by all of this because I was stoned and in a fight with my soon-to-be-ex boyfriend and still didn't see a common ground between my extreme immature ways and Nick's responsible farm-boy persona. I went over by the drum set and sat with my friend Sam while he laid down a groove to some guy playing Bach on the piano.

And then in a stroke of genius, I set Nick up with a writer friend of mine from New Jersey who thought he was cute, and together with Rob we formed a nice little squad. It was really great, because it opened up all of these opportunities for me to hang out with Nick in a low-pressure situation and learn about his love of Taylor Swift and John Mayer, and become more aware that he wasn't a super weirdo like all of the other single men I knew in New York. Even though I rooted for him and my friend to hit it off, it didn't happen and YoU'lL nEvEr BeLiEvE wHaT hApPeNeD nExT.

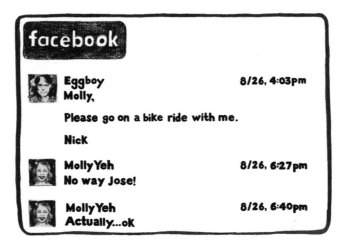

Eggboy
8/26, 4:03pm
Molly,

Please go on a bike ride with me.

Nick

MollyYeh
8/26, 6:27pm
No way Jose!

MollyYeh
8/26, 6:40pm
Actually...ok

. . . was my extremely flaccid attempt at being sassy before agreeing to a 4 a.m. departure time that Tuesday.

The night before I was a little nervous because I genuinely had no idea if this was just a friendly presunrise hangout or a date date. But through some good old-fashioned high school–style sleuthery, Rob informed me that I should probably treat this like a date and not dress like a slob. So I wore high-rise denim shorts, a sweaty pink T-shirt, and ratty old Toms. I've never known how to dress for dates, ever.

At 4:30 a.m. the next day, I emerged from my door to find a smile that was entirely too bright for such an early morning; and even for such a cynical time in my life, it was magnificent. I had zero expectations, no intention of becoming his girlfriend or fiancée or wife at the time, not even a concern over maintaining our years-long acquaintanceship for much longer, as I lived in Brooklyn and he lived a good hour away in Washington Heights. But as I slumped down the steps, the part of my brain where nostalgia is kept knew to burn that smile into my memory, just in case. (I know, that's really mushy and weird, but it actually happened!)

We biked over about 12 bridges, through 20 miles of Brooklyn, into Queens, and eventually to Rockaway Beach, where we sat on the sand and swatted a team of very violent flies away from fruits and croissants while we discussed all of our favorite things and who we still kept in touch with from Juilliard. We even discussed politics, which is my least favorite thing to talk about ever, but somehow he got it out of me in a way that didn't make me want to throw sand in my eyeballs. It wasn't just Rob's warning the night before, it was the surprise fruits and croissants he brought along that gave away the dateness of it all. *Had he known that the Peter Bjorn and John song "Paris 2004," where they sing about fruits and croissants, is one of my all-time favorite songs???*

Throughout our ride, I never got butterflies or nerves, just a shocking sense of calmness that doesn't exist naturally in New York. Nick's patience and lack of ego were disarming, and it was clear as day that he could care less about Cronuts, Twitter, any sort of a scene or trend at all, really. I never felt the need to impress him with my fancy restaurant knowledge and he didn't ask me once if I had read any *New Yorker* articles. He liked *Andy Griffith* and carried around a small vial of dirt from his farm. His family members were his closest friends. He was a country bumpkin to the extreme, and an 80-year-old trapped in a young body that was more Zac-Efron-circa-*High-School-Musical* than *The Lucky One*.

When we returned to my apartment, I set a carton of eggs on the counter and told him to make something while I took a shower and got ready for my afternoon job at Juilliard's newspaper. I put on a pink button-down shirt printed with mice and cheese all over it and an officey skirt and returned with wet hair to a plate of partially scrambled, very well-done eggs covered with dried basil and nothing else. He told me I looked nice and I told him his eggs were undersalted. "It's okay, there's actually no salt on them," he said almost proudly, before admitting that he had no idea how to properly scramble an egg. And actually, these were "marbled eggs," not scrambled eggs, and they were meant to be superior because they skipped the step of beating the eggs

before they hit the pan, in the name of using fewer dishes. It was all so wildly endearing, and I choked them down while he explained his egg-centric diet to me. How he paired dozens of eggs with kettle-bell workouts in hopes of breaking out of the skinny frame that he'd always had, and how he normally also added oregano but could only find basil in my spice drawer.

The next day we hung out again because from the beginning there was an unspoken rule that dating rules didn't apply to us, and we went out for dinner with Rob and the girl he was dating that day. It was the night before Rob and I were leaving for a weekend at adult summer camp, so I had made plans to crash on his couch so we could leave easily the next morning. As the four of us sat outside at a restaurant on the Upper West Side, I watched Rob become a heightened version of his typical goofy self, complete with his over-the-top quirky humor and all of his best jokes. Nick discreetly let me order for the both of us so that I could have half of two things I wanted from the menu instead of the entirety of one, and that was pretty much the moment when I realized we were a thing and that I wouldn't ever have to dig up all of my best jokes for a night of impressing. That was cool, because I don't have any jokes.

I ordered hummus and a goat cheese salad for us. And I ate *a lot* of that hummus. Like, all of that hummus. And it was the stupidest thing I've ever done in the history of ever because later that night, as Nick, my future husband, smooched me for the very first time in the middle of Rob's high-rise apartment in Lincoln Center while Rob walked his date home to 96th Street, I farted the loudest fart I've ever farted in all of my life.

It wasn't a nightmare, it wasn't a drill, it wasn't one of those silent but deadly farts that you can get out of if you draw attention to another part of the room; it was the sound of me ruining all of my chances with a good honest dignified human being. I wanted to pull my butt off and die by way of not having a butt.

I still can't eat hummus without thinking about it.

But luckily, as Rob assured me time and time again at camp, Nick was worth dating because he doesn't care about silly things like farts.

After camp Nick and I were inseparable, and keen on the morning dates, when we could drink all of my roommates' coffee and eat eggs in every possible form. One by one, I went down my list of best ways to prepare eggs in order to contribute to his Zac-Efron goals and teach him what was beyond his world of marbled eggs. Slow scrambled, poached, you know, the standards. I showed him his first egg cup and how to eat a soft-boiled egg and he gobbled them up so fast that when it came time to finally acknowledge the person that was suddenly lurking in the back of all of my blog photos, "Eggboy" was born.

HUMMUS

Makes 2½ cups

Let's just say that the fact that I continue to eat so much hummus despite my having to relive that hummus farting nightmare each time is a testament to how good it is, *when made correctly.*

In America, it's easy to grow up believing that putting things like artichokes and pesto and (omg) the liquid from the chickpea can in hummus is okay, but one trip to Israel or at least one bite of warm hummus made with good, deeply nutty tahini and the round earthy flavor of freshly cooked chickpeas should be enough to convert you. You know me, I love a good twist on a classic, but when it comes to hummus, I am a purist with the commandments of my culinary hero, Janna Gur, burned into my brain:

1. Chickpeas should be soaked overnight and then boiled until they're very soft before going into hummus.

2. Hummus consists of chickpeas, lemon juice, tahini, salt, and maybe garlic.

3. It should be at room temperature when you serve it, or still warm from the cooked chickpeas.

After my first trip to Israel, when I finally got around to doing the chickpea soak and boiling the little beans, Eggboy was so bowled over that he's been ruined for cold acidic grocery-store hummus ever since. We like our hummus the consistency of mousse, which will come about after a couple of minutes in a good food processor. And we like it at all hours of the day, but I especially like it for breakfast, just like how I had it in Israel. It's a filling way to begin the day, and also that way if it causes any, um, tummy trouble, you'll have the whole day to walk it off before you see your significant other, or potential significant other, that night.

A few quick things:

• The baking soda helps the chickpeas break down and achieve their softest potential, which leads to a smoother hummus. It's also supposed to decrease the gassy effects of chickpeas, but it's all too sensitive of a subject for me to test.

• The quality of your tahini makes or breaks the quality of your hummus. (See my tahini notes on page xviii.)

• At the very least, serve your hummus with a layer of good olive oil on top. Store it that way too, so the top doesn't dry out. For a fancy-pants hummus that doesn't involve all

(recipe continues)

the dipshit ingredients that big brands in America like to add, top your hummus with a puddle of tahini sauce, chopped onion, parsley, and maybe some spicy *zhoug* or a hard-boiled egg. Or check out the Hummus with Meat All over It (page 169).

• Don't go 90 percent in and then wuss out for the last 10 percent. Make sure you're eating this with equally good pita (see the recipe on page 24).

1 cup dried chickpeas

½ teaspoon baking soda

1 tablespoon lemon juice

½ cup tahini

¾ teaspoon kosher salt, plus more to taste

2 cloves garlic (optional)

¼ cup cold water

Olive oil, for drizzling

Tahini Sauce (recipe follows), for serving

Finely chopped onion (for topping) and onion wedges (for dipping)

Chopped fresh flat-leaf parsley, for serving

Freshly baked Pita (page 24), for serving

Other Fun Toppings

Zhoug (recipe follows)

1 large hard-boiled egg, sliced

In a medium bowl, cover the chickpeas with enough water to reach 2 inches above the height of the chickpeas and soak them for 12 hours.

Drain and rinse the chickpeas and place them in a large saucepan with the baking soda. Cover them with 1 to 2 inches water and bring the water to a boil over high heat. Reduce the heat to low, cover the pot, and simmer until the chickpeas are very soft, about 2 hours. Drain them and let cool slightly, then transfer to a food processor.

Add the lemon juice, tahini, salt, and the garlic (if using) and blend until very smooth, about 1 minute. With the motor running, drizzle in the water and continue to blend for 2 to 3 more minutes. Taste and season with additional salt if needed.

Transfer to a serving dish, top with a drizzle of olive oil, the tahini sauce, chopped onion, and parsley. Serve with fresh pita and onion wedges for dipping, and zhoug and a hard-boiled egg, if desired, and enjoy.

Any leftovers should be stored in an airtight container in the fridge with a thin layer of olive oil coating the top.

Use within 3 days.

TAHINI SAUCE

Makes 1/2 cup

1/4 cup tahini

3 tablespoons cold water

1 tablespoon lemon juice

Kosher salt and black pepper

In a small bowl, mix together the tahini, water, and lemon juice until the mixture thickens. Season with salt and pepper to taste.

ZHOUG

Makes 1 1/2 cups

5 jalapeños, seeded and coarsely chopped

4 cloves garlic

1 bunch flat-leaf parsley, coarsely chopped (about 1 cup)

1 bunch fresh cilantro, coarsely chopped (about 1 cup)

1 teaspoon ground cumin

1/2 teaspoon ground coriander

1/4 teaspoon cayenne pepper

1/2 teaspoon kosher salt

Black pepper

1/4 cup olive oil

In a food processor, combine the jalapeños, garlic, parsley, cilantro, cumin, coriander, cayenne, salt, a few turns of pepper, and the olive oil and blend until it's the consistency of pesto, adding more olive oil if desired. Store in the fridge for up to 3 days or spoon into ice cube trays, freeze, and thaw as needed.

PITA

Makes 12 pitas

Pita should be a thick, fluffy disk of warm bread that would make the ultimate sleeping bag if ever we entered real-life *Honey, We Shrunk Ourselves*. One dunk of this into some fresh hummus, and you'll be ruined for the store-bought kind.

1½ cups warm water

2¼ teaspoons (1 envelope) active dry yeast

1½ tablespoons sugar

1½ teaspoons kosher salt

3 tablespoons olive oil

3¾ cups bread flour (see Note), plus more for dusting

In a stand mixer fitted with the dough hook, mix together the water, yeast, and sugar. Let it sit for 5 minutes, or until foamy. With the mixer running on low speed, add the salt and oil, then gradually add the flour. Increase the speed to medium-high and mix until the dough is smooth and slightly sticky, 7 to 10 minutes, adding just enough additional flour so that the dough no longer sticks to the bowl. Place the dough in an oiled bowl and turn it once or twice to coat it in oil. Cover the bowl with plastic wrap and let it rise at room temperature until it has doubled in size, about 2 hours.

Turn the dough out onto a clean work surface and divide it into 12 equal pieces. Mold each piece into a ball by stretching the top and tucking the edges under. Place the balls 1 inch apart on a piece of parchment paper, cover them with plastic wrap, and let them rise for 30 minutes.

Preheat the oven to 500°F. Line two baking sheets with parchment paper.

With a rolling pin, roll out the balls of dough into rounds, ¼ inch thick. Place them on the baking sheets and bake until cooked through and puffy, about 5 minutes. I prefer them quite doughy, so I don't allow them to brown in the oven (knowing that they'll brown slightly when reheated in the toaster), but feel free to keep them in the oven for a few minutes longer if you'd like them browned. Cool on a rack and enjoy.

Leftovers can be frozen in an airtight container or zip-top bag and then reheated in the microwave or toaster.

Note: Sub in 1¾ cups whole wheat flour for 1¾ cups of the bread flour, if desired.

SHAKSHUKA COUSCOUS

Makes 4 servings

Teaching Eggboy the pronunciations of my favorite foods was probably as amusing for me as it was for him to teach me what a combine is. There's a certain specialness in watching a grown man pronounce "schnitzel," "babka," and "za'atar" for the first time; but perhaps the best new word I taught him was *shakshuka*. Mostly because he loves eating it as much as he loves saying it, yielding a very staccato and excited pronunciation.

Eggboy avoided eating gluten for a time, and so for a while we turned to this tomato and egg dish as a go-to brunch or dinner. All of the ingredients are pretty easy to have on hand at all times, except for maybe the parsley, and truth be told, if it's just the two of us I usually get lazy about adding it. But I do love making this for guests since it's a beautiful dish that can be easily scaled depending on how many people are coming over, and it's great any time of year.

What makes this one different from the thousand million shakshukas that exploded onto the Internet in like 2012 is that somewhere along the way in development, Eggboy made a peculiar suggestion of adding couscous to it. Remember, Eggboy doesn't really cook, and so whenever he makes a cooking suggestion it's either really really bizarre ("Chicken Pot Babka") or worth checking out. Luckily this was the latter, and it's proved to be satisfying as a breakfast, brunch, lunch, or dinner.

However long you have to make your shakshuka, that is how long you should take. If you're having a hurried morning but in the mood for something warming and comforting, you can bang this out in 10, maybe 15 minutes. If it's harvest season and your husband is out in the fields and you have *no* idea how long it will be before he gets in but you want to make him his favorite dish in the whole wide world because maybe you got in a fight and it was all your fault, then simmer the sauce over low heat until the cows come home. And then when he says that he'll be home in half an hour, wait 5 minutes, crack in your eggs, and let them cook for, oh, say the 45 minutes that it actually does take him to get home. You'll have a mind-blowing flavor bomb of a stew with egg yolks that have the consistency of softened butter.

(recipe continues)

3 tablespoons olive oil, plus more for drizzling

1 medium yellow onion, chopped

Kosher salt

3 cloves garlic, minced

1 tablespoon ground cumin

1 teaspoon harissa, or more to taste (different brands vary in spiciness)

¼ teaspoon smoked paprika

Black pepper

Crushed red pepper

1 tablespoon tomato paste

1 can or carton (28 ounces) chopped tomatoes

1 teaspoon sugar

¾ cup Israeli couscous (optional)

½ cup vegetable broth (optional)

4 large eggs

½ cup crumbled feta cheese

A handful of chopped fresh flat-leaf parsley

In a large skillet, heat the 3 tablespoons of oil over medium heat. Add the onion and a pinch of salt and cook, stirring, until soft and translucent, 5 to 7 minutes. Add the garlic, cumin, harissa, smoked paprika, a good pinch of salt, a few turns of black pepper, and a pinch of red chili flakes and cook until it's all dreamy smelly, about 2 minutes. Stir in the tomato paste, then the chopped tomatoes and sugar. If you're hungry and short on time, crank the heat up and go on to the egg step (and nix the couscous and broth). If you're patient and have the time, bring the mixture to a simmer, reduce the heat to low, stir in the Israeli couscous and broth , and simmer this sauce, covered, for at least 25 minutes or until the couscous is cooked, up to 1 hour or so, stirring occasionally. Add additional broth to thin the mixture if desired.

Taste the sauce and add what you believe is right.

Create 4 little wells and crack in your eggs. Either baste the eggs by spooning the hot tomato sauce over them, or just let them be in a sunny-side-up situation. When the whites are cooked but the yolks are still runny, remove from the heat. Sprinkle the eggs with a little salt and black pepper, drizzle with olive oil, top the whole pan with feta and parsley, and serve.

A TRIO OF SPREADS

With better timing and more gall on my part, his nickname would have been Nutboy, because what supplements his dozens of eggs are jars and jars of almond butter and peanut butter. He adds a large heaping spoonful of it to all things, even his eggs (?!?!). So the fact that I'm not so much the jam-making farm wife and more the food processor-wrangling nut-toasting wife goes well with this. Eggboy's typical nut butter of choice contains just roasted nuts and salt, which makes homemade versions as easy as dumping a bunch of nuts in a food processor and blending while I check Instagram for 5 to 10 minutes. But here are a few special occasion spreads that are smooth, sweet, and useable anywhere you'd use Nutella.

All three of these can be stored at room temperature and when they're packaged in jars with fun little labels, they make great gifts.

MARZIPAN BUTTER

Makes 1 cup

It turns out that if you take the basic ingredients of marzipan and blend them for longer than you've ever blended anything in your life, you get a stunning silky spread that looks deceptively like white chocolate and tastes exactly like marzipan. The fun part about this recipe and the following pistachio butter recipe is watching the patterns of the nuts getting ground up in the processor. First they turn to crumbs, then they get clumpy, then they form a massive clump, then they get kind of spready, then they might get clumpy again, and eventually they just let their oils alllllll hang out, and over the hum of the processor motor you can hear the sound of lips smacking and that's how you know that butter is being made. Don't even think about attempting this if you don't have a reliable workhorse of a processor. I still use my mom's old Cuisinart that's probably twice my age and it's great, but I'm convinced that if it ever breaks, it'll be because of this marzipan butter. It'll be worth it, though.

2 cups blanched almonds (8 ounces)

¾ cup powdered sugar

¼ teaspoon salt

1 teaspoon almond extract

In a food processor, blend the almonds, scraping the sides occasionally, until creamy and spreadable, 10 to 12 minutes. Add the powdered sugar, salt, and almond extract and blend, scraping the sides occasionally, until very creamy, 12 to 15 more minutes. Caution: The mixture will be quite hot when it's finished blending.

CHOCOLATE HALVA SPREAD

Makes ¾ cup

Here's a nut-free morning spread that's inspired by a popular toast topping in Israel, made from mixing honey or date honey with tahini to make spreadable halva. This version subs out the honey for chocolate to make the Middle Eastern cousin that Nutella always yearned for.

⅔ cup (4 ounces) chopped milk chocolate or milk chocolate chips

½ cup tahini

⅛ teaspoon kosher salt

½ teaspoon vanilla extract

Melt the chocolate in a double boiler or by microwaving in 30-second increments, stirring after each, until melted and smooth. Stir in the tahini, salt, and vanilla. It will thicken as it cools.

WHITE CHOCOLATE PISTACHIO BUTTER

Makes a little more than ½ cup

Does anyone want to explain to me why it's so easy to find peanut butter, almond butter, and sunflower seed butter, but not pistachio butter? It's so cool and green, like a fancy slime. Can I offer you some fancy slime toast?

Again, just like with the marzipan butter, don't make this without a reliable food processor.

1 cup unsalted roasted pistachios

½ cup white chocolate chips

1 tablespoon sugar

⅛ teaspoon kosher salt

½ teaspoon almond extract

½ teaspoon vanilla extract

In a food processor, combine the pistachios, white chocolate chips, sugar, salt, almond extract, and vanilla and blend, scraping the sides occasionally, until very creamy and spreadable, about 10 minutes.

ISRAELI BREAKFAST

If our gold '05 Buick LeSabre doubled as a teleporting device, I would most often use it to go to breakfast in Israel. Eggboy and I would order mountains of fresh salad filled with crisp sweet cucumbers and bright juicy tomatoes and we'd cover it all with tahini and za'atar and chase it with dollops of labneh and fluffy puffy pita dunked in hummus. We'd wave good morning to the beach before hurrying back for our workdays on the farm.

Oh, you guys! Breakfast in Israel is the best. There is no other time and place when I've ever been so excited about (wait for it . . .) *vegetables*. The flavorful bright salads they serve for breakfast there are actually life-changing. They're not lettucey or spinachy, they're mostly chopped salads, heavy on the tomatoes and cucumbers, and *herbs!* I'll tell you, that country knows a thing or two about fresh herbs.

A great part about salad for breakfast is how it delivers an early sense of accomplishment akin to running 5 miles in the morning. Not that I'd know what that really feels like. But imagine starting your day with a bowl of the most beautiful vegetables in the world, and then going about your day knowing that you've already fulfilled most of your recommended daily servings of vegetables. The possibilities of what to do from there are endless: You could eat cake and not feel guilty! You could eat more vegetables and be superman because they're just that good! You could do both!

I've only been to Israel thrice, always in the summer, and when I come back, I eat chopped tomatoes, cucumbers, and onions by the ton, until the first frost. The sweet vegetables in Israel are practically vegetable royalty, they're so good; but in the summer, when Eggboy's tending our garden, our veggies can hang pretty well.

Every morning over the summer, when the ground is still dewy, I slip my Birkenstocks on and scamper out in my PJs to pull a couple of tomatoes and a cucumber before sprinting back in, to minimize the mosquito damage (they are relentless motherfuckers up here). Inside, I stand at my counter, seeding and chopping tomatoes and cucumbers, tossing them with a little salt, and then draining them as I chop the onion. Any fresh herbs that I've yanked from the ground get finely chopped too. The whole process is as therapeutic as morning yoga. And because I can't make a good cup of coffee to save my life, this is as close to a daily morning ritual as I'll ever come.

I could eat Israeli breakfast every single day, for three meals a day, it's that good. It's about as different from my childhood breakfasts as humanly possible, but I like this new tradition that's healthy and uses all of our garden vegetables. I just wish that it wouldn't have to be limited to our short summer months.

Israeli Salad

1. Combine These

1 part
Chopped Red Onion

2 parts
Chopped Tomato

2 parts
Chopped Cucumber

2. Toss with

Fresh Lemon Juice

Black Pepper

Kosher Salt

Extra Virgin Olive Oil

optional
(but recommended)

Sumac

Thyme

Za'atar

Flat-leaf Parsley

Fresh Cilantro

MY EVERYMORNING BREAKFAST
FOR THE SUMMER

Makes 1 serving

This is essentially how I turn my morning salad into a meal. I place it on a bed of yogurt, drizzle it with tahini, make it rain za'atar and sumac, and then use a big spoon to help it onto a slice of bread or pita. If I'm really in need of a fill-up, I'll top it all with a fried egg. It is such a nice sunny start to the day!

¼ cup plain Greek yogurt or labneh
(full-fat preferable, but not necessary)

2 teaspoons olive oil

Kosher salt and black pepper

½ cup Israeli Salad (page 34)

1 tablespoon tahini

A fried egg (optional)

Za'atar

Ground sumac

Bread, for serving

Spread the yogurt on a plate or bowl. Drizzle it with the olive oil and sprinkle with a pinch of salt and a few turns of pepper. Top with the Israeli salad, the tahini, and a fried egg (if desired), and sprinkle on a few good pinches of za'atar and sumac. Serve with bread.

KALE KHACHAPURI

Makes 4 servings

This dish is basically the best kind of breakfast pizza (the breakfast pizza that's got a runny egg on it, not the breakfast pizza that's cold leftovers from the refrigerator, although that's super good too), but with a shape that's more conducive to holding a runny egg. It's the iconic shape of the Georgian cheesy bread, *khachapuri*. And while a traditional khachapuri wouldn't have kale in it, the alliteration is as fun to say as it is to eat. The other stars of this show besides the kale and egg are tangy labneh and a really honorable amount of garlic. Mmm breath.

2 tablespoons olive oil, plus more for serving

8 ounces chopped kale

Kosher salt and black pepper

4 cloves garlic, thinly sliced

Flour, for dusting

Pizza Dough (page 120)

1 cup Labneh (recipe follows)

1 cup shredded Parmesan cheese

4 large eggs

Za'atar, for serving

Tabasco sauce, for serving

Preheat the oven to 500°F, with a pizza stone if you have one.

In a large skillet, heat 2 tablespoons oil over medium-high heat. Add the kale, ¼ teaspoon salt, and a few turns of pepper and cook, stirring, until the kale is wilted, about 5 minutes. Add the garlic and cook for 2 more minutes. Remove from the heat and set aside.

Place a piece of parchment paper on a pizza peel, if using a pizza stone, or a baking sheet and dust it with flour. Divide the dough into 4 portions. Working with one portion at a time, flatten out the dough into an 8-inch round. Spread with ¼ cup labneh, leaving a 1-inch border. Top with 3 tablespoons Parmesan and one-quarter of the kale, leaving a 2-inch well in the center. Pinch up two opposite sides to create a boat shape, and sprinkle with 1 more tablespoon Parmesan.

Bake for 4 minutes. Open the oven and then quickly pour an egg into the kale well (this is easiest if you crack it first into a small bowl or glass and have it ready to pour). It's okay if some of the whites overflow. Bake until the whites are firm but the yolks are still runny. Begin checking for doneness at 5 minutes. Drizzle with olive oil and sprinkle with a pinch of za'atar, a pinch of salt, and a turn of pepper. Repeat with the remaining dough. Serve with Tabasco.

LABNEH

Makes just under 2 cups

Labneh is a tangy Middle Eastern cream cheese that is silkier than the cheese you have on bagels. It's equally at home under a pile of fresh vegetables in the morning as it is drizzled with olive oil and sprinkled with za'atar and lapped up with a happy-hour flatbread. If you live someplace fancy like New York or San Francisco (or actually maybe any place that has a Whole Foods), perfectly respectable labneh is a grocery-store trip away, but yada-yada-living-in-the-middle-of-nowhere, we make our own. And, okay, full disclosure: I don't always have my act together to accomplish the two steps it takes to prepare labneh the night before, so I often catch myself calling plain full-fat Greek yogurt labneh. With a bit of salt, they're nearly interchangeable; but going the extra mile and draining your already-drained yogurt will yield a sturdier spread that's more worthy of the title of "cheese."

1 quart plain full-fat Greek yogurt

¼ teaspoon kosher salt

1 teaspoon lemon juice

Olive oil and za'atar or other seasonings as desired, for serving

Pita (page 24), for serving

In a large bowl, mix together the yogurt, salt, and lemon juice. Line a colander with three layers of cheesecloth and place the colander over a large bowl. Pour the yogurt into the cheesecloth, cover the whole thing with plastic wrap, and set the bowl in the refrigerator for 8 hours or overnight, emptying the liquid in the bowl as needed. If you're not using it in a recipe, you can serve it on its own. Top with a big splash of olive oil and additional seasoning and serve with pita. Store in an airtight container in the fridge.

CARDAMOM ORANGE KUBANEH

Makes 1 loaf

If a croissant bought a gym membership and started bulking up its muscles so that it was no longer a delicate flaky pastry but a hunky filled-out Chris Hemsworth–type, that would be *kubaneh*. Kubaneh is a buttery, layered Yemeni bread that is traditionally slow-baked overnight on Shabbat and enjoyed for Saturday morning brunch with grated fresh tomato and hard-boiled eggs. I don't think I met a single person in Israel who didn't have a Yemenite neighbor growing up whose grandma made it every week. Just mentioning kubaneh would send their lips smacking and their eyes to the back of their head.

Typically kubaneh is made of your basics: flour, water, salt, sugar, yeast, and butter (or margarine, for a parve alternative). But the sucker requires time and ideally a special kubaneh pot (see Note), and while baking it slow and low is the traditional route, slow cooker directions are also included here and will yield almost identical results.

The following gives a nod to my Scandinavian neighbors with a bit of cardamom and also to my mom who often poured orange juice in her white bread dough. It's a very untraditional kubaneh that will make your house smell like IKEA while producing a slightly sweeter loaf reminiscent of cinnamon swirl bread. It's excellent on its own, with jam, or a slathering of cream cheese or labneh.

1¼ cups warm water

¼ cup orange juice

2¼ teaspoons (1 envelope) active dry yeast

3¼ cups flour, plus more for dusting

1 teaspoon kosher salt

2 teaspoons grated orange zest

½ cup sugar

2 teaspoons ground cinnamon

½ teaspoon ground cardamom

½ cup unsalted butter, at room temperature

In a medium bowl, combine the water, orange juice, and yeast and give it a little stir. Let it sit for about 5 minutes, until it becomes foamy on top.

Meanwhile, in a large bowl (or in a stand mixer fitted with a dough hook), mix together the flour, salt, orange zest, ¼ cup of the sugar, 1 teaspoon of the cinnamon, and ¼ teaspoon of the cardamom.

(recipe continues)

When the yeast is foamy, add it to the dry mixture and stir to combine. Knead by hand on a floured surface (or with a dough hook) until you have a smooth and slightly sticky dough, 7 to 10 minutes, adding more flour as necessary (but try not to add too much).

Transfer the dough to an oiled bowl, cover it with plastic wrap, and let it sit at room temperature until it has doubled in size, 1 to 2 hours.

To make the filling, stir together the butter and the remaining ¼ cup sugar, 1 teaspoon cinnamon, and ¼ teaspoon cardamom.

To shape the loaf, turn the dough out onto a lightly floured surface. Divide it into 5 equal parts. Working with 1 part at a time (leaving the remaining parts covered), pat it out or roll with a rolling pin into an 8 x 5-inch rectangle. Spread it with a layer of filling, roll it up lengthwise like a jelly-roll, then coil it up like a snail and spread the outside with a thin layer of the butter mixture (this can get a little messy! But it doesn't need to be perfect). Place it in a kubaneh pot (see Note for alternatives) and repeat with the remaining dough and filling, placing the rolls snugly together. Any leftover butter should get distributed on top of the dough. Proceed below to the oven method or slow cooker method.

Oven method: Cover the pot with a tight-fitting lid or wrap it tightly with foil (or both if the lid is loose) and let the dough rise for an additional 30 minutes. Preheat the oven to 225°F and bake for 6 hours. Let cool slightly and enjoy.

Slow cooker method: Cover the pot with a tight-fitting lid or wrap it tightly with foil (or both if the lid is loose) and place it in a large slow cooker. Set the slow cooker to low and cook for 6 hours or overnight. Let cool slightly and enjoy.

This bread is best enjoyed immediately but can be reheated in the oven the next day with the lid on. Bake at 225°F for 30 to 45 minutes.

Note: A kubaneh pot is a high-sided lidded aluminum pot about 7 inches wide. Without one, you can get by using an ovenproof 2½- to 2¾-quart vessel (such as a Dutch oven), either with a lid or wrapped tightly with a few layers of foil.

SOFT BOILED EGGIE

SESAME COFFEE CAKE!!

LEMON POPPY SEED OLIVE OIL MUFFINS

CHOCOLATE MARZIPAN SCONE LOAF

THE LADIES
OF GRAND FORKS
BRUNCH CLUB

I had my camera, my kitchen, and Netflix Christmas movies. Those were my friends when I moved to town. Oh! And sometimes we went to the Ruby Tuesday with the Eggparents. It was just about everything I needed to recover from the sensory overload that built up over 6 years in New York.

I was living that life and stinking up a storm. Every day I came closer to mastering the art of IDGAFing by not showering and allowing my hair to turn into dreads. I enjoyed a solitary life that didn't require me to get dressed in grown-up clothes and run a brush through my hair in order to look presentable enough to go out in public. But when I finally came to and realized that I'd have to shave my head if I didn't start taking care of my person, I also decided that I should probably get friends.

In New York when you want friends, you attend highly specific events like the New Music Bake Sale or a panel discussion on Roman Jewish cuisine, and then stick around for the schmoozing afterwards. Or you wear a loud garment onto the train and cold-compliment someone who is wearing a similar one. Or you track down any of your dozens of former high school or summer camp friends who have also moved to the city and make plans to catch up with them. Or, hell, you go to the synagogue on 88th Street and even though your new friend might end up proposing to you the following week, you've still had some kind of human interaction. It's all really easy, making friends in New York. Wildly easy.

The story is a little different in Grand Forks, North Dakota, where everybody has known each other since childhood. Their parents have known each other since childhood and their grandparents, too. Meeting new people is a muscle that's not often flexed, so the process of making friends here was different and sometimes scary.

Eventually I slowed down and learned to let go of the urgency I exercised in New York that required me to learn the profession, birthplace, career goals, and relationship status of every new person I met. I softened like a slow-cooked brisket and experimented with getting to know people by osmosis. I learned by just being around them, observing their ways, and letting them take the lead for achieving friendship statuses like Instagram friends and Juicy Gossip Text Message friends. Maybe silently analyzing my new friends' every move was a little creepy, but I just didn't know how to act around all of these new people.

Ultimately it was through a post that I wrote for Food52 that I got a few emails from some hip local ladies who expressed an appreciation for dim sum, brunch, and sarcasm. I tried with all of my might not to screw things up with my new acquaintances and found myself executing my new patient social skills. The training wheels were off and we didn't have mutual friends or common work places to connect over. I stood on the sidelines, exercising light banter until I settled into the rhythm of their humor, and over time I picked up on the small details that back in New York I'd have to know in 5 minutes. Only by then their numbers of siblings and neighborhoods where they lived didn't seem to carry so much weight because what mattered was that I had made friends with some really great people.

I knew I'd really made it when we formed a club. A brunch club! Because the brunch options in Grand Forks are limited to crowded diners that follow the no-booze-before-noon-in-North-Dakota rule. But we don't stand for that, no ma'am. We are quiche-baking, mimosa-drinking, cheese-loving ladies who brunch, and boys aren't technically allowed but we make exceptions if there are extra waffles. We don't brunch every weekend, but when we do, it's filled with a lot of eggs and a lot of baked goods.

SESAME COFFEE CAKE

Makes one 8-inch cake

I am obviously a fan of anything that gives you the right to eat cake for breakfast. Even if it does have a very misleading name. Where is the coffee in coffee cake, hm?? What would happen if we started naming all of our foods with the drinks that we're meant to have with them? Can I interest you in some beer pizza? A lemonade hot dog? That's what I thought.

Luckily, coffee cake has the redeeming factor of sugary-buttery-crumbly shit all up in it that is so great, I could eat a bowl of that alone.

This coffee cake is heavy on that crumbly shit and has two nontraditional additions of sesame and *hawaij*, a cardamomy Yemeni spice blend that deserves to be in your coffee more than pumpkin spice (see Hawaij Hot Chocolate, page 248). I recommend making this the day you're going to serve it because ooh, girl, warm coffee cake and hot coffee is a winter morning dream.

Topping

¾ cup flour

½ cup lightly packed light brown sugar

¼ teaspoon kosher salt

½ teaspoon ground cinnamon

½ teaspoon Hawaij for Coffee (recipe follows)

6 tablespoons unsalted butter, at room temperature

2 tablespoons toasted sesame seeds

Cake

1½ cups flour

1 teaspoon ground cinnamon

1 teaspoon Hawaij for Coffee (recipe follows)

1 teaspoon baking powder

½ teaspoon baking soda

½ teaspoon kosher salt

½ cup unsalted butter, at room temperature

⅓ cup tahini

1 cup sugar

1 large egg

1 large egg yolk

2 teaspoons vanilla extract

½ cup sour cream

Preheat the oven to 375°F. Grease an 8 x 8-inch baking dish.

To make the topping: In a medium bowl, whisk together the flour, brown sugar, salt, cinnamon, and hawaij. Using a wooden spoon or your hands, mix in the butter until combined and crumbly. Mix in the sesame seeds. Set aside.

(recipe continues)

To make the cake: In a medium bowl, combine the flour, cinnamon, hawaij, baking powder, baking soda, and salt and whisk to combine. In a stand mixer fitted with the paddle attachment, cream together the butter, tahini, and sugar until pale and fluffy, 3 to 4 minutes. Add the whole egg and egg yolk and mix to combine, then beat in the vanilla. Mix in half of the flour mixture, add the sour cream, then mix in the remaining flour mixture.

Scrape the batter into the baking dish and spread it out evenly. Sprinkle the topping evenly over the batter. Bake until a toothpick inserted into the center comes out clean. Begin checking for doneness at 35 minutes. Make sure that it is done before taking it out of the oven, otherwise the center will sink! Serve warm out of the pan.

HAWAIJ FOR COFFEE

Makes 4½ tablespoons

If you're just making this to go in your coffee cake, feel free to make a half batch. HOWEVER, I'd advise against it because any leftovers should be kept on hand to sprinkle into your morning coffee grounds (or Hawaij Hot Chocolate, page 248) for a delightful warming experience.

Combine These

½ tsp ground nutmeg

2 tb ground cardamom

2 tb ground ginger

½ tsp ground cloves

½ tsp ground cinnamon

DARK CHOCOLATE MARZIPAN SCONE LOAF

Makes 1 loaf

I grew up believing that it was normal to wake up on Sundays to freshly baked scones and coffee cakes. My mom is a freak with the baked goods. She loves bringing home new cookbooks from the library and testing out any and all of the good-lookin' baked goods. She's the reason I never saw baking as a scary intimidating thing, but rather a really fun thing that's worth waking up before sunrise on a Sunday for.

Baking for other people has long been my way of telling people that I think they're pretty cool. (It was easier said than done when I started dating Eggboy, though, because back then he was gluten-free.) So I make sure that there's at least one baked good at every Brunch Club meeting, and sometimes we end up with seven and that's fun too.

In its infancy, this recipe was for classic triangular jam-filled scones that were inspired by the beautiful scones on Sarah Kieffer's *Vanilla Bean Blog*. Since I live for marzipan, I threw in some chopped marzipan and chocolate chips and began making scones that farmers in the area were saying were the best they'd ever had. But in their small scone shape, they were only really great the day of, and I wanted something that would last a little longer than that. Enter: the scone loaf! It's just a massive scone with a crust that helps retain its moisture long enough so that you can make it the day before your brunch party if you'd like. Cut it with a very sharp knife to avoid it crumbling everywhere and serve with a slathering of jam.

7 or 8 ounces marzipan, chopped into ½-inch pieces

1 tablespoon powdered sugar

½ cup dark chocolate chips

2 cups flour, plus more for dusting

1 tablespoon baking powder

½ teaspoon kosher salt

2 tablespoons plus 1 teaspoon sugar

¾ cup cold unsalted butter, cut into ½-inch cubes

2 large eggs

½ cup buttermilk or heavy cream

½ teaspoon vanilla extract

½ teaspoon almond extract

Jam, for serving

Preheat the oven to 400°F. Line an 8 x 4-inch loaf pan with parchment paper, allowing 1-inch wings to hang over the edges on the long sides.

In a large bowl, toss together the marzipan and powdered sugar to coat. Add the chocolate chips and set aside.

In a food processor, combine the flour, baking powder, salt, and 2 tablespoons of the sugar and pulse to combine. Add the butter cubes and pulse until the butter is the size of peas. Add this to the bowl with the marzipan.

In a small bowl, whisk together the eggs, buttermilk or cream, and extracts and add to the dry ingredients. Use a wooden spoon or spatula to stir until just combined.

Pour the mixture into the prepared loaf pan and spread it out evenly. Sprinkle the top with the remaining 1 teaspoon sugar and bake until golden brown on top and a toothpick inserted into the center comes out clean. Begin checking for doneness at 40 minutes.

Cool in the pan on a wire rack for 10 minutes. Using the parchment wings, remove to the rack to cool completely. Slice with a serrated knife and serve with jam.

DUKKAH DONUTS
WITH BLOOD ORANGE GLAZE

Makes 12 donuts

The only all-nighter I ever really pulled was in the name of donuts. It happened in college when after a night of suffering through megaphone poetry in Washington Heights and watching my friends dance the salsa on the Lower East Side, it was decided that we should probably just kill 2 hours at the Yaffa Cafe (RIP) once the bars closed so that we could get to the Doughnut Plant when it opened. This was around the time when I was anxious that the world was going to end before I could try all of the donuts in Manhattan.

I was so proud of myself for convincing my friends of this plan that I ordered one of each flavor and together, my two friends, some guy from Alaska, and I ate 14 of the doughiest glaziest donuts in the city. Miraculously none of us puked and I made it uptown to orchestra rehearsal on time for the downbeat of Schoenberg's Five Pieces for Orchestra. Ah, to be resilient after all-nighters again. . . .

My donuts these days are all homemade, as we don't have any donut shops in town, unless you count a Tim Hortons that mainly caters to the Canadian population that descends upon Grand Forks on the weekends to go to Target.

Frying them is typically reserved for Hanukkah (see Rosemary Sufganiyot, page 201), but for the rest of the year I use my trusty baked donut pan. It took me a while to warm up to baked donuts, pegging them as nothing but fraudulent muffins, but they're pretty darn tasty in that quirky shape of theirs. These have a density level somewhere between a cupcake and a muffin and they're coated with the Egyptian nut and seed mix, *dukkah,* which gains a certain specialness thanks to a heavy dose of coriander and anise. Oh, and I am such a sucker for alliteration! Aren't you?

Donuts

1¾ cups flour

1 cup sugar

1 teaspoon baking powder

½ teaspoon baking soda

¾ teaspoon kosher salt

1 large egg

½ cup buttermilk

¼ cup flavorless oil

1 teaspoon vanilla extract

¼ cup water

Glaze

3 cups powdered sugar

2 tablespoons honey

4 to 5 tablespoons fresh blood orange juice (about 2 blood oranges)

(recipe continues)

Dukkah

Combine These ↘

1/4 C hazelnuts
toasted and coarsely ground

A pinch of kosher salt

1/4 C toasted
sesame seeds

1 tb coriander seeds,
toasted and
coarsely ground

1 tb ground
anise seeds

To make the donuts: Preheat the oven to 375°F. Coat a 12-cavity donut pan with cooking spray.

In a large bowl, whisk together the flour, sugar, baking powder, baking soda, and salt. In a medium bowl, whisk together the egg, buttermilk, oil, vanilla, and water. Whisk the wet mixture into the dry mixture and stir to combine. Fill a piping bag (with no tip) with the batter and pipe the batter into the donut cavities, filling each halfway. This could get a little messy.

Bake until a toothpick inserted into a donut comes out clean, about 12 minutes. Cool in the pan for 5 minutes, then remove to a wire rack to cool completely.

To make the glaze: In a small bowl, mix together the powdered sugar, honey, and 4 tablespoons orange juice. Add more juice little by little until the mixture is spreadable (you might not need the full remaining tablespoon). It should be quite thick yet spreadable.

To decorate the donuts, dip them halfway into the glaze and then allow excess glaze to drip off. Sprinkle the tops with dukkah and enjoy.

BAKED EGGS WITH POTATOES AND ZA'ATAR

Makes 8 servings

Growing a love of casseroles was an easy thing for me to do as a new upper-midwesterner (see Hotdish, page 144). They're so good, they're easy to transport, and they can feed a lot of people. This breakfast variety is a hybrid of a Spanish tortilla, a quiche, and a thing called "egg bake," which is common up here and typically involves store-bought hash browns. Boiling thinly sliced potatoes in a pool of olive oil (like you would if you were making a Spanish tortilla) makes the potatoes smooth and buttery, which blends so well with the custardy base of a quiche. The best part about this is the leftovers, though. (That's the best part of any casserole, right?) They reheat wonderfully, so when you have them, let them cool, slice into individual portions, wrap individually, and store in the fridge. Reheat throughout the week for a quick breakfast, either by itself or between two slices of bread for a breakfast sandwich.

2 cups olive oil

1½ pounds russet potatoes, unpeeled and thinly sliced (⅛ inch thick)

1 large onion, thinly sliced

1¼ teaspoons kosher salt

Black pepper

8 large eggs

¾ cup whole milk

½ cup heavy cream

1 tablespoon za'atar

1 teaspoon sweet paprika

3 ounces white cheddar cheese, grated

Greek yogurt or labneh, for serving

Preheat the oven to 400°F.

In a large skillet, heat the olive oil over medium heat. Add the potatoes and onion and bring the oil to a low boil. Simmer the potatoes, stirring often, for 15 minutes. Drain the potatoes and onions into a colander, catching the excess oil in a heatproof bowl. Reserve a few tablespoons of the oil to grease your baking dish and save the rest of it for future use.

Season the potatoes with the salt and a bunch of turns of pepper. In a separate medium bowl, whisk together the eggs, milk, cream, za'atar, and paprika. Pour the egg mixture over the potatoes and onions, add the cheddar, and fold everything together.

Coat a 13 x 9-inch baking dish with the reserved olive oil and pour in the mixture. Bake until set and browned on top. Begin checking for doneness at 30 minutes. Let cool slightly and serve with yogurt or labneh.

FRESH MINT ICED COFFEE

Makes 1 serving

Fancy coffee drinks are stupid and anyone who contaminates their coffee with anything besides more coffee/an espresso shot/ice is someone who deserves a little bit of side-eye. That is what my mom raised me to believe, and for further proof you can go visit her between the hours of sunrise and noon, when she has the largest glass of iced coffee you've ever seen glued to her hand. There's a straw sticking out of it, of course; it's how her teeth stay so white.

So I've always been a black coffee person. I always will be.

But the exception to this rule is a drink that I was introduced to at Philz Coffee, in Berkeley. Muddled fresh mint leaves, ice, cold brew, simple syrup, and cream. Have you ever brushed your teeth and then felt that buttery satisfying sensation of drinking iced coffee immediately after? This is exactly that but intensified by a trillion. The combination is beyond your wildest dreams. It's like 1 + 1 = 7. I don't know how it happens, it's so magical and I can't make sense of it. I don't even want to, because it's a *fancy coffee drink*. But I have no choice. Just do it.

4 fresh mint leaves

Ice

1 cup freshly brewed strong coffee

1 tablespoon heavy cream

1 tablespoon simple syrup (recipe follows)

Muddle the mint leaves in a large glass. Fill it with ice. Pour in the coffee, heavy cream, and simple syrup, and give it a little swirl. Enjoy!

SIMPLE SYRUP

Makes 1¼ cups

1 cup sugar

1 cup water

In a small saucepan, whisk together the sugar and water and bring to a boil, stirring often. Remove from the heat and let it cool. Transfer to a container and store in the fridge for up to 2 weeks.

LEEK AND SWISS MINI QUICHES

Makes 12 servings

I have always loved quiche, and I'm thinking that maybe it makes up for the fact that when it comes to dessert, I am on Team Cake, *not* Team Pie. A slice of quiche, queen of the savory pies, paired with a lightly dressed mesclun salad is one of the more perfect brunches, I'd say. It's the type of thing that you just need a little of in order to feel satisfied and in the style of the '70s.

My favorite way to make quiche involves purposely buying way too much dough and then snacking on the leftovers while the quiche bakes. The weird flavor of raw store-bought pie dough always brings me back to hanging out with my mom and Stoopie while they made quiche Lorraines, which was a common occurrence in our house. (I have two favorite Lorraines, quiche and Lorraine McFly from *Back to the Future*.)

These mini quiches are vegetarian sisters to Lorraine, with sweet delicate leeks in the place of bacon. They're great hot or at room temperature

2 tablespoons unsalted butter

2 large leeks, finely chopped

Kosher salt

3 large eggs

½ cup heavy cream

⅛ teaspoon ground nutmeg

¼ teaspoon sweet paprika

¼ teaspoon cayenne pepper

Black pepper

2 teaspoons Dijon mustard

3 ounces Gruyère or Swiss cheese, shredded

1 package (14 to 15 ounces) refrigerated pie dough, or homemade pie dough of choice

Preheat the oven to 375°F. Coat 12 cups of a muffin tin with cooking spray.

In a skillet, melt the butter over medium-high heat. Add the leeks and a pinch of salt and cook, stirring often, until soft and translucent, 7 to 10 minutes. Remove from the heat and set aside to cool.

In a medium bowl, whisk together the eggs, cream, nutmeg, paprika, cayenne, a few turns of black pepper, the mustard, and ¼ teaspoon salt. Stir in the cheese and leeks.

Divide the dough into 12 equal parts and roll into small balls. Roll each of them out into a 4½-inch round and press them into the muffin tins, crimping the edges if desired.

Divide the egg mixture among the muffin cups and bake until set. Begin checking for doneness at 30 minutes. Let cool slightly and serve.

CHALLAH WAFFLES AND BRUNCH BRISKET

Makes 8 servings

The first time I traveled out of the country was when I was 8 and my dad took Stoop and me to the International Clarinet Festival, which was happening in Belgium that year. The parts I remember most vividly can be grouped into two categories: food I ate and loved, and naked things I saw. The naked things just had to do with going to the beach and seeing how normal it was for lady boobs to be out in the open, and then of course there was the Manneken Pis fountain, which is a statue of a small boy holding his winky, which is where the water comes out.

Food I loved in Belgium included chocolate, sandwiches with butter *and* salami, and waffles. I had had those big round waffles before in the States, but the chewy yeast-risen Liège waffles really had an impact on me. They were so much more flavorful and satisfying, and it bewildered me that of the two main types of Belgian waffles, these were the types that got left behind when waffles made the trip to the States.

A decade later, with some inspiration from the Wafels & Dinges truck in New York, I hunted down the secret ingredient to make them from scratch, Belgian pearl sugar. These magical crunchy pebbles of sweetness are what make Liège waffles unique, and they're probably best ordered on Amazon. (Swedish pearl sugar, a slightly smaller variety, will also do the trick.)

I'm using a challah-ish dough here, since it is my comfort dough, and it's paired with a brisket in a dish that's inspired by chicken and waffles. Both of these do their magic overnight, so if you're wanting to throw a wild brunch, take a few minutes to stir together a dough and stick it in the fridge, then throw some stuff in your slow cooker. Go to bed, and when you wake up, all you'll need to do is press a few waffles.

Brunch Brisket (recipe follows)
Challah Waffles (recipe follows)

Make the brisket the day before (or at least 8 hours before serving if making the day of).

Make the waffle dough the day before (or at least 4 hours before serving if making the day of). Set up the waffle maker and make the waffles as instructed in the recipe (keep them warm in a low oven if making ahead).

To serve, top a waffle with brisket and gravy, if using, and enjoy!

(recipe continues)

CHALLAH WAFFLES

Makes 8 large or 16 small waffles

2¼ teaspoons (1 envelope) active dry yeast

¾ cup warm water

1 teaspoon plus ¼ cup sugar

1 teaspoon kosher salt

3½ cups flour

2 large eggs

½ cup flavorless oil, plus more for greasing the waffle iron

2 teaspoons vanilla extract

½ teaspoon almond extract

1 cup Belgian or Swedish pearl sugar

In a medium bowl, combine the yeast, warm water, and 1 teaspoon of the sugar and give it a little stir. Let it sit for about 5 minutes, until it becomes foamy on top.

Meanwhile, in a stand mixer fitted with the dough hook, mix together the salt, flour, and remaining ¼ cup sugar. In a separate medium bowl, whisk together the eggs, oil, vanilla, and almond extract.

When the yeast is foamy, add it to the dry mixture immediately followed by the egg mixture and knead with the dough hook until the dough is smooth and slightly sticky, 7 to 10 minutes, adding flour as needed. Transfer the dough to an oiled bowl, cover it with plastic wrap, and let it rise until doubled in size, either at room temperature for 2 hours or in the refrigerator overnight.

If refrigerating the dough, let the dough sit at room temperature for 1 hour before proceeding.

On a lightly floured surface, knead the pearl sugar into the dough and then divide it into 8 to 16 balls, depending on how big you'd like your waffles. Heat up your waffle iron, brush it with oil, and cook the balls of dough until browned and cooked through. Keep the dough covered until it's used. If you're not serving these immediately, hold them in a warm oven.

BRUNCH BRISKET

Makes 8 servings

This is Bubbe's brisket dressing up as breakfast sausage for Halloween, brown sugar and all. If you don't have a slow cooker, allow breakfast brisket to be the reason you get one (but see the Note).

1 brisket (3 pounds)	1 tablespoon dried sage
2 teaspoons kosher salt	1 teaspoon dried thyme
Black pepper	1 teaspoon dried rosemary
2 tablespoons flavorless oil	2 cups low-sodium beef or vegetable broth
1 large onion, thinly sliced	1 large apple, cut into thin wedges
½ teaspoon crushed red pepper	2 tablespoons packed light brown sugar
¾ teaspoon cayenne pepper	1 cup red wine
½ teaspoon ground nutmeg	1 can (14 ounces) diced tomatoes
½ teaspoon fennel seeds	¼ cup flour (optional; to make a gravy)
A pinch of ground cloves	

Season both sides of the brisket with the salt and a few turns of pepper.

In a large skillet or pot, heat the oil over medium-high heat. Sear both sides of the brisket until browned, 4 to 6 minutes. Transfer it to a slow cooker.

Add the onion to the skillet and cook, stirring, until soft, 5 to 7 minutes. Add the crushed red pepper, cayenne, nutmeg, fennel seeds, cloves, sage, thyme, and rosemary and cook, stirring, for 2 more minutes. Pour ½ cup broth into the pan and allow it to loosen any browned bits stuck to the bottom of the pan (use a spatula to help scrape them up). Pour the whole mixture into the slow cooker.

Add the apple, brown sugar, wine, tomatoes, and remaining 1½ cups broth to the slow cooker. Cover and cook on low for 8 to 10 hours, or overnight. Remove the brisket to a cutting board and let it sit for 15 minutes. Trim off any excess fat, shred the meat, and then transfer it to a serving dish. Carefully pour the mixture from the slow cooker on top of the brisket and serve. Or, if you'd like to make a gravy, strain out 2 cups of the liquid and place it in a saucepan over medium heat. Gradually whisk in the flour and stir until thickened.

Note: As an alternative to the slow cooker, cook everything in a covered baking dish or Dutch oven in a 325°F oven until very tender, 3 to 4 hours.

BRUSSELS SPROUT RÖSTI

Makes 8 servings

Here's something I just made up: If you call a latke a rösti, you don't have to wait until Hanukkah to eat one. You don't even have to wait until sundown. Not that you *have* to wait until Hanukkah to make latkes, but sometimes I get all purist about these things in the interest of keeping the holidays special, so it's not often that you'll find a classic latke in my house until Hanukkah.

But this is hardly a classic latke!

Remember in 2013 when Hanukkah and Thanksgiving aligned and the Internet nearly shat itself with mash-up recipes to tha NINES? American Jewish food bloggers everywhere came armed with challah stuffing and latke pumpkin pie, and cranberry sauce was stuffed into every single *sufganiyah* orifice in existence. History was made, mistakes were made, it was the single greatest food event in American Jewish food blogger history.

This recipe is based on one of my contributions to Thanksgivukkah that has lived on past all of that jazz. Brussels sprout latkes with balsamic Dijon sour cream (lightened up here with yogurt) were a mix of the classic potato latke and the Dijon-soaked Brussels sprouts that my mom makes every Thanksgiving. They're the Brussels sprouts that made me love Brussels sprouts, because until then they were the gross evil villains that fell from the sky in *Cloudy with a Chance of Meatballs*.

Please enjoy this latke for the everyday.

4 large egg whites

1 tablespoon lemon juice, plus more for serving

4 cups lightly packed finely shredded Brussels sprouts (about 12 ounces)

1 medium onion, finely chopped

2 cloves garlic, minced

¾ cup flour or chickpea flour

Kosher salt and black pepper

1 teaspoon crushed red pepper or Aleppo pepper

Flavorless oil, for frying

Balsamic Dijon Yogurt (recipe follows)

In a large bowl, whisk together the egg whites and lemon juice. Add the Brussels sprouts, onion, and garlic and stir to combine. Stir in the flour, ¾ teaspoon salt, a lot of turns of black pepper, and a few pinches of crushed red pepper or Aleppo pepper.

In a large skillet, heat a thin layer of oil over medium-high heat until shimmering. Using an ice cream scoop, scoop in about one-eighth of the Brussels sprout mixture and use a spatula to pat it out into a pancake. Cook on both sides until browned, 3 to 4 minutes on each side.

Remove to a plate lined with paper towels, sprinkle with salt and a squeeze of lemon, and serve with balsamic Dijon yogurt.

BALSAMIC DIJON YOGURT

Makes about 1¼ cups

1 cup plain full-fat Greek yogurt

2 tablespoons Dijon mustard

2 tablespoons honey

1 tablespoon balsamic vinegar

¼ teaspoon kosher salt

In a medium bowl, mix together the yogurt, mustard, honey, vinegar, and salt.

SCALLION PANCAKES AND MAPLE SYRUP SLAW

Makes 8 servings

Here is my version of pancakes and syrup! It's a very tasty hangover brunch dish that lends itself well to being topped with a fried egg and maybe some chopped thick bacon; but really it's good at all times of the day and night. It consists of a classic scallion pancake, aka my guiltiest pleasure when ordering Chinese takeout, and its hot salty chewy crispiness is met with a cold, crunchy, sweet, refreshing maple carrot slaw for a dish to appeal to everything happening in your mouth. And this shit's vegan!

I've been making these since my Brooklyn days, when I'd persuade my roommates every few weeks to allow me to host concerts and art installations in our apartment for a secret supper club called the Pacific Street Table and Stage. My artist friends would arrive with their instruments and costumes to workshop new tunes and sing about grilled cheese; and under a string of lights we'd drink Two-Buck Chuck and eat dumplings and scallion pancakes. The nights were smoky and the music was loud and there were never any leftover scallion pancakes.

If you'd like to make the pancakes ahead of time, you can form them and roll them out and then wrap them tightly in plastic wrap and freeze. They can be put in a hot pan straight from the freezer, just be sure to fry them for longer.

Maple Syrup Slaw
2 tablespoons soy sauce

¼ cup maple syrup

½ cup rice vinegar

1 teaspoon minced fresh ginger

4 cups shredded carrots

Scallion Pancakes
2 cups flour, plus more for dusting

1½ teaspoons kosher salt

1 teaspoon baking powder

1 cup water

Filling
3 tablespoons toasted sesame oil

Black pepper

5 scallions, very finely chopped

Crushed red pepper

Flavorless oil, for frying

1 tablespoon toasted sesame seeds, for serving

1 scallion, finely chopped, for serving

To make the slaw: In a large bowl, mix together the soy sauce, maple syrup, vinegar, and ginger. Add the carrots and toss to coat evenly. Cover and refrigerate for at least 30 minutes or overnight.

To make the pancakes: In a large bowl, mix together the flour, salt, and baking powder. Stir in the water to form a dough. Knead the dough on a lightly floured surface until it is smooth and slightly sticky, about 10 minutes, adding more flour as necessary. Cover the dough with a damp kitchen towel and let it sit for 20 minutes.

To fill the pancakes: Divide the dough into 4 equal parts and keep them covered when you're not working with them. Working with 1 piece of dough at a time, roll out a 7- to 8-inch round. Brush it evenly with a thin layer of sesame oil and top with a few turns of black pepper, one-quarter of the chopped scallions, and a good pinch of crushed red pepper. Roll it up like a jelly-roll and then coil the jelly-roll into a spiral snail shape. Roll that out into a 7- to 8-inch round. Repeat with the remaining dough and filling.

In a large skillet, heat ⅛ inch oil over medium-high heat until shimmering. Fry the pancakes for a few minutes on both sides until golden brown. Transfer to a plate lined with a paper towel.

To serve, cut each pancake into wedges. Top with the carrot slaw, toasted sesame seeds, and scallions.

II
MAINS
(& SOME OTHER FUN STUFF)

JUILLIARD

I tuned the timpani incorrectly, that's why I cried after my Juilliard audition. I sobbed right into a bowl of macaroni and cheese at the Chat 'n Chew in Union Square and later all over the Coach store on Fifth Avenue with my best friend Nathan because I had blown my chances of getting into my dream school. For as long as I can remember, hitting things has been my mode of choice for creating sound, ever since I discovered the joys of striking my mom's pots and pans with the spoons and whisks. Rhythm is in my bones, and this manifested in a love of classical music and the gift of a marimba for my 16th birthday instead of a car.

When it came time to apply to college, I had long known that I wanted to follow in my dad's footsteps at his alma mater and pursue my fantasies of moving to New York to spend my days playing the tambourine, and I had never worked so hard for something in my life.

So three weeks later, when I pulled into the parking lot of the Des Plaines, Illinois, golf range with my high-school boyfriend Michael and the jingle jingle of my phone showed a call from Juilliard during the week when calls went out to admitted students (indicating that I hadn't blown my audition after all), all of the tears went in reverse order back into my eyes.

That fall I moved to New York to study music, oblivious of the fact that 4 years later I would stay for the food.

Together with the two other percussionists admitted that year, Sam and Dave from New Jersey, we forged our way into the little family of percussionists who were already there. We spent our lives on the third floor of the school, in the compound of percussion practice rooms that were connected by little pathways lined with octaves of button gongs and bins marked "cowbells" and "shaker things." Some of the instruments looked like indigenous works of art; others had belonged to percussion legends of the past. It was like a museum and a playhouse rolled into one, and later at times a hellhole of stress, home to difficult practice sessions that extended long past midnight and made me question what was so wrong with me that I couldn't retain atonal vibraphone runs or the muscle memory needed to play flawless xylophone octaves. But we were pretty good at partying off all of the stress on the weekends, usually at parties in fifth-floor walk-ups in Harlem, usually on nights that ended with the Recession Special at Gray's Papaya on 72nd Street (two hot dogs with sauerkraut and relish and a papaya juice).

I racked up musical performances whose memories still sit glowing in the back of my mind like shiny hidden treasures, like Berio's *Circles,* which Sam and I brewed up in record time, Reich's *Music for 18 Musicians* with Steve Reich in attendance, and Mahler 5 at Carnegie Hall with he-who-would-later-become-Eggboy across the stage on trombone. My part in the Reich was three chords on the marimba, struck over and over and over for more than an hour, but standing in the center of that stage as a train of sound barreled slowly across time while I did my part to help it move along, was like being high in the potato chip aisle.

I loved that high and I wanted it all the time. (A trumpet player once told me that a coke addiction can achieve this! Don't worry, Ma, I never tested that.) The thing about being a percussionist though is that composers didn't start giving us much heavy lifting until well into the twentieth century. Beethoven, Brahms, and Bruckner have all forced percussionists to sit through hours of rehearsals and concerts for the sake of a few triangle notes. Yeah, I know, there are worse places to sit than the back of a stage while an orchestra serenades you with iconic symphonies of the past, but for me it started to get frustrating; I wondered what opportunities I was missing.

I daydreamed about what I could be accomplishing if I could just pass off my few triangle notes to a violinist and leave to go do other things. And in rehearsals during so many hours counting rests before I'd even get to play, I'd spend my time avoiding being flashed by the other percussionists and, I don't even know, reading easy books that didn't require a whole lot of energy to focus on so that I could keep one eye on the conductor.

So I determined early on in my time at Juilliard that being in a professional orchestra wouldn't make me happy. This left open a much more amorphous window, with

RECESSION SPECIAL

space for potential things like gigs on Broadway, with chamber groups around the city, and in recording studios. I didn't like that this wasn't as straightforward and, in the long run, as secure as the orchestra path, but the more I sat bored in the back of the orchestra, the more I learned what I wanted.

Meanwhile, I was anything but bored in my private lessons. Gordon, my teacher, had a personality so bright I needed sunglasses and a Red Bull to keep up. He entered the room to the tune of imaginary big bands and always had tales to tell of his recent culinary adventures. Our lessons began before I even auditioned at Juilliard, at his studio near Union Square, in the same building where I'd later interview to be the personal assistant to his neighbor, Jeffrey Steingarten. I knew immediately that Gordon was who I wanted to study with, and over time, it became clear that there was a lot more to that than keeping perfect time.

Gordon was a part of the Gastronauts, a vaguely illegal dinner club that hosted meals centered around ingredients like pythons and lamb brains. When our snare drum lessons were over, he told me about civet cat coffee, the coffee ground from beans that get eaten and pooped out by a cat. And then on one especially impressionable afternoon, he discussed the Minetta Tavern Black Label Burger (which at the time was *only $26*) in such precise detail that I had no choice but to spend all of my work-study money that night on a table for one at the Minetta Tavern. Gordon was the reason I fought for a reservation at Momofuku Ko and the first person to ever explain wine to me.

This all happened during my third year at Juilliard, the one when I was determined to figure out exactly what I'd do after graduation; but the excitement and intrigue of this new world of food kept getting in the way. I started my blog that year and moved out of the dorms into my first apartment, on West 96th Street, and discovered that writing about a burger or making a batch of cupcakes and arranging them on my three-tiered IKEA plate and blogging about it gave me a high that was so oddly similar to playing Steve Reich. I thought I had cheated a system in place that says you need to go through a little more hell before you can feel that good, but really I had just found something else that I loved to do.

I began taking gigs around the city in new-to-me neighborhoods just so that I could explore the food in those areas. Like, I didn't totally care for the opera workshop on the far west side of the island, but I powered through in the name of a *torta* from the back of Tehuitzingo on 47th Street. Or what got me excited about the choral gigs in Morningside Heights were thoughts of the post-show ramen at Jin up on 125th. And then on days off when I wasn't out and about tasting the city's newest donut, I baked up storms in my tiny kitchen, ran experiments on slow-poached eggs, and started a mustard collection that took over the refrigerator.

I blogged all about it, I blogged up a storm. I used my tiny point and shoot camera to take pictures of dumplings I invented in the dim orange light of my windowless living room and I wrote to whoever would read it (my mom). What got me thrilled about food and blogging was how I could create something that was all my own from start to finish and I could be in control. I had never been able to do that with music; it was always other people's music that I was just interpreting, and writing music was never something I could grasp. But a recipe and a blog post? That I could do.

Eventually this portion of time that was devoted to doing these new things took enough pressure off of my musical studies for me to remember why I was studying it in the first place. It's good! Music is so good! My first few years of shredding excerpts and putting pressure on myself to play them perfectly mechanically had burnt me out on music, but taking time off to do other things allowed me to reapproach it with a clearer mind. I processed the fact that I didn't want to be in an orchestra or freelance all the time, but music was in me and it wasn't leaving. From there I moved forward with my relationship to music in the way that ex-boyfriends who aren't devils at the core really can turn into friends.

In order to graduate, all of the musicians at Juilliard have to play a senior recital. I was excited about mine because for years I had been keeping a list of all of my favorite pieces, and my recital was my chance to put them all together. I threw myself into the planning process as heavily as I'd prepared for my entrance audition, lining up a mix of whimsical music written by composer friends and challenging creepy half-naked pieces that I was afraid to perform for my extended family but knew I had no choice. I opened with a Nico Muhly solo that required a cage of instruments and a bit of sweat, performed a goofy piece written for an old Nintendo console, and then closed with one of the most hauntingly beautiful pieces in all the repertoire, George Crumb's *Music for a Summer Evening*. Oh, that piece! It brings me to tears every time. It's a 40-minute trance of ghostly prepared pianos and bowed gongs that sound all at once alien and nostalgic. In the very end, this big broody bear of sound walks slowly, slowly away, turning around only for a few final quintuplets of laughter, but getting softer and softer until a low soft tam tam note is one last big hug goodbye.

When I graduated, I wasn't exactly sure what was next but the wonderful tiny team at the Juilliard newspaper took me in and offered me a part-time job that allowed me to stay in New York, write, and take whatever other gigs the city presented me, in music or in food.

I loved my time at Juilliard. It was exciting, inspiring, and more than anything, it taught me how to work. I wouldn't have traded it for all of the pizza in New York. But sweet Jesus, if you made me repeat it all over again I'd chop off my hands.

Becoming Schnitzel

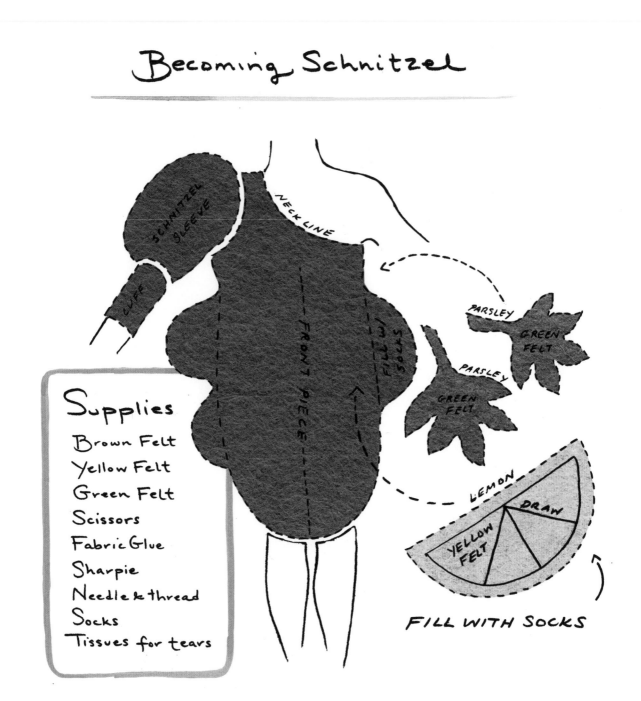

SCHNITZEL SLEEVE

CUFF

NECK LINE

FRONT PIECE

FILL W/ SOCKS

PARSLEY
GREEN FELT

PARSLEY
GREEN FELT

LEMON

DRAW

YELLOW FELT

FILL WITH SOCKS

Supplies
Brown Felt
Yellow Felt
Green Felt
Scissors
Fabric Glue
Sharpie
Needle & thread
Socks
Tissues for tears

SCHNITZEL BAO WITH SRIRACHA MAYO AND SESAME PICKLES

Makes 12 bao

For a while in high school, my mom and I were really good at finding excuses to eat schnitzel. "Aw shucks, you didn't do well on your test? Will schnitzel make you feel better?" or "Oh yay! You aced your test! Let's celebrate with schnitzel!" or "No school today? Let's eat schnitzel!" We found a reason in every life event to drive two towns over to Kuhn's Delicatessen for a glorified chicken nugget squeezed with a wedge of lemon, and no matter what the occasion was, schnitzel always delivered. It's like duct tape, it fixes everything even if it's not broken.

So when I moved to New York, I found my bank, my Duane Reade, and my schnitzel spot. The Schnitzel & Things truck remains one of the best schnitzels in the city, and it is responsible for one of the single tastiest months of my life. In July 2010, I finagled my way into becoming the truck's 5,000th Twitter follower and a month of free schnitzel was my prize. (I should admit that followers number 4,990, 4,991, 4,992, etc., were the accounts @mollyyeh1, @mollyyeh2, @mollyyeh3, and so on and so forth.) As if an entire month of schnitzel wasn't enough, I was also an unpaid magazine intern living in New York at the height of its food truck obsession, so I had hit the jackpot.

Every day during my lunch hour at *Time Out*, I would take my rickety brown bike and zoom across Midtown, snaking through traffic and dodging car doors like fireballs. I was like a video game superhero hunting down the golden schnitzel, wherever it was hiding that day. A cape might have been appropriate. I worked my way systematically down the menu, trying every item and every combination of sauces and sides. They schnitzeled chicken, veal, cod, and eggplant . . . there was even a schnitzel burger that I think was a deep-fried burger. It was so insane, all of it. I don't think I ate anything else that month because their schnitzel was the size of my head and came on beds of the best ciabatta in the city. I loved their schnitzel with spicy mayo and extra hot Dijon.

I was schnitzel for Halloween that year, naturally. At midnight the night before, I sat in my bedroom and hand-sewed a brown lumpy one-sleeved fitted dress that I stuffed with socks so that the lumps would jut out. I attached a large felt lemon wedge to the shoulder next to a sprig of green felt parsley. I only broke down in ugly tears twice that night! The next day at Sam and Dave's Halloween party no one knew what I was. In their eyes, I was a Long Island iced tea or Mr. Hankey the Christmas Poo with lemon on it. *Flips hair* All of my friends were losers that night.

(recipe continues)

This schnitzel variation is a nod to my Chinese side and comes nestled in steamed *gua bao*, or "taco buns," as they're more commonly referred to in our house. Premade versions are found precisely nowhere in the upper Midwest, so I've included a way to make them from scratch using the dough from A Pair of Nice Buns (page 198); but if you can get them at your local Asian market, going that route is just fine. These buns are a dangerous combination of salty, squishy, sweet, sour, crunchy, spicy, and mayo-y.

Sesame Pickles

½ cucumber or 2 Persian cucumbers, thinly sliced (ideally with a mandoline)

½ teaspoon crushed red pepper

1½ teaspoons sugar

1 tablespoon rice vinegar

2 teaspoons soy sauce

2 teaspoons toasted sesame oil

Schnitzel

Flavorless oil, for deep-frying

½ cup flour

2 large eggs, lightly beaten with 2 tablespoons water

2 cups panko breadcrumbs

Kosher salt and black pepper

1 pound boneless, skinless chicken breasts, cut into 12 equal pieces

Lemon wedges

Assembly

12 steamed gua bao, store-bought or homemade (page 200)

Sriracha mayo (¼ cup mayonnaise mixed with 2 teaspoons Sriracha sauce, or to taste)

To make the pickles: In a medium bowl, mix together the cucumber, crushed red pepper, sugar, vinegar, soy sauce, and sesame oil. Cover and refrigerate until ready to use.

To make the schnitzel: Pour 1½ inches of oil into a large heavy pot or high-sided skillet. Clip on a deep-fry thermometer and heat the oil over medium-high heat to 360°F.

Set up a dredging station: Place the flour, eggs, and breadcrumbs in each of three separate bowls. Season the breadcrumbs with 1 teaspoon salt and a few turns of pepper.

Place a piece of chicken between two large pieces of plastic wrap and use a rolling pin or other blunt object to pound the chicken until it is as thin as you can make it without it tearing. Repeat with the remaining chicken. Coat the chicken in flour, egg wash, and breadcrumbs and fry in batches, flipping once, until golden brown, 2 to 3 minutes. Transfer to a paper towel to drain and season both sides with salt and pepper and squeeze with lemon.

To assemble: Spread the insides of a bao with Sriracha mayo and fill with a piece of schnitzel and a few pickles.

SPINACH AND FETA RUGELACH

Makes 16 rugelach

For better and for worse, Juilliard was an itsy-bitsy community of 800 students from all over the world, but mostly New Jersey and Asia. All of the rehearsals, classes, and offices were in one building in Lincoln Center that was five stories above the ground and five stories below, and had little hidden treasures throughout, like a wig shop where students could get cheap haircuts and a very well-stocked candy bowl in the head of chamber music's office. It wasn't uncommon to run into visiting artists like Gustavo Dudamel or Lang Lang, and once I was snooping around the fifth-floor orchestra room when I was drafted to teach a B-list *Sesame Street* character how to play the crash cymbals for a taping with Alan Gilbert. It was a really exciting place to be, and a major thing that I learned early on was that going to school in sweatpants like I did every day in high school wasn't going to fly.

In Mary Anthony Cox's ear training class, I sat in the same seat in the same room that my dad had sat in 30 years prior, and though she'd normally address everyone with "now, honey," she slipped once and nearly called me by my dad's name. Juilliard was a home and a family. There were practice rooms to hide in if you needed a good cry, but everyone always knew what was up, so truly hiding your stress was never really an option. It was smothering at times, but on most days I was grateful for the familiarity of it all because being away from my actual family wasn't always easy.

Often I'd get care packages from my mom that included tchotchkes for my dorm room and always a batch of her rugelach or cookie bars. I probably could have hoarded them in my mallet bag and no one would have noticed, but I loved the excuse to deliver them all over and schmooze with my friends. The arrival of Jody's Rugelach was a really good reason to sit in the dance and percussion hallway and commiserate about a difficult music history quiz or the vibraphone passage with awkward stickings.

My mom's rugelach are typically filled with chocolate chips and cinnamon sugar. And if that's what you're looking for, head over to Molly O'Neill's *New York Cookbook,* because that's my mom's go-to recipe. This is my savory twist on rugelach that, full disclosure, started off as a spinach pop tart. When my mom was testing the recipe though, she "accidentally" rugelach-ed it and created what's in my opinion, a much better ratio of crust to spinach.

The filling on its own is also really good! It's a cheesy creamed spinach that's kind of janky because I'm never in the right mindset to actually cook the frozen spinach

(recipe continues)

block and drain it before adding it to the pot; but if that grosses you out you can get rid of the liquid beforehand. It actually doesn't make a big difference here.

Also! Leftovers make a really great breakfast or snack when reheated in a toaster oven.

10 ounces frozen chopped spinach

2 tablespoons unsalted butter

1 small onion, finely chopped

Kosher salt

2 to 4 cloves garlic, minced

Black pepper

2 tablespoons flour

3 tablespoons heavy cream

¾ cup crumbled feta cheese

1 teaspoon lemon juice

A few shakes of hot sauce

1 package (14 to 15 ounces) refrigerated pie dough, store-bought or homemade

1 large egg yolk, beaten with a splash of water

Flaky sea salt

Preheat the oven to 425°F. Line two baking sheets with parchment paper. Set the frozen spinach out on a plate at room temperature to soften slightly.

In a large pot, melt the butter over medium heat. Add the onion and a pinch of salt. Cook, stirring often, until the onion is soft and translucent, 5 to 7 minutes. Add the garlic and a few turns of black pepper and cook for 1 more minute, until fragrant. Add the flour and stir to combine, then stir in the heavy cream. Give the frozen block of spinach a rough chop and stir it into the pot with a good pinch of salt. Cook, stirring, until the spinach is heated through and the mixture is combined. Stir in the feta, lemon juice, and hot sauce and then remove it from the heat. Taste and adjust seasonings as desired.

Roll out half of the dough on a lightly floured surface until it is a large round, about ¼ inch thick. (If using store-bought pre-rolled dough, simply unroll it onto your surface.) Spread on half of the spinach mixture in an even layer so that it covers the dough. Using a pizza cutter or knife, cut the dough like a pizza into 8 triangular wedges. Roll up each section starting at the wide end. Transfer the rugelach to a baking sheet, placing them 1 inch apart. Repeat with the other half of the dough and spinach filling.

Lightly brush the tops with the egg wash and sprinkle with sea salt.

Bake until golden brown, about 20 minutes. Let cool slightly and enjoy.

Store leftovers in the fridge and reheat in a toaster oven.

SPAGHETTI AND MY EX-BOYFRIEND'S MEATLESS BALLS

Makes 4 servings

During my second year of college, I dated a vaguely macho Philly-based vegetarian who survived almost entirely on cheese and beer and Rita's wuhter ice. We had met at a summer orchestra festival at the University of Maryland and bonded over spiking our slushies before rehearsals and eating cheese sandwiches from the hippie food co-op in the basement of the student union. When we returned to our respective cities at the end of the summer we did the duty of schlepping back and forth via BoltBus in the name of Young Love. (Which is a terrible idea because Philadelphia and New York are jusssst close enough that you think you can get away with a quick 12-hour round trip, but in practice that requires more sleep deprivation than is acceptable for a day of long rehearsals.) On my weekends in Philadelphia we'd usually play xylophone excerpts for each other, as he was always preparing for the next big orchestra audition, and I was still dabbling with the idea of taking some auditions. Then we'd venture off to Monk's for a beer bought with Stoopie's old ID, and a bucket of Belgian french fries. They were nice little adventures away from the City, because compared to New York, even just going to Philly felt rejuvenating and relaxing. But the best weekends were when we'd unwind at his parents' house in the suburbs, which brought about the two main components of his legacy that remain in my life today: his dad's wondrous latkes (see page 204) and his mom's meatless meatballs.

This guy was a real curious type of vegetarian in that you'd rarely catch him eating fake meat or beans or vegetables, but his mom's fake meatballs were the absolute tits and everyone knew it. They were dense and flavorful and so perfect that if they had been invented before actual meatballs, you'd think that actual meatballs were trying to impersonate them. Typically they were served at parties in red sauce with toothpicks as an appetizer, but I probably made a meal out of them on more than one occasion.

In the years after our breakup, my desire to relive these balls eventually transcended any negative ex-y feelings and made the awkward Facebook conversation to acquire the recipe 100 percent worth it. There was no beating around the bush with formalities, I just dove into the trenches of ex-boyfriend territory, went for the meat, so to speak, and came back with this here recipe for you.

(recipe continues)

This version has been tweaked slightly from the original and includes my favorite way to turn the balls into a meal (with soft white spaghetti). But try stuffing them into a hoagie or putting them out in a slow cooker for a party, and see how many people can catch that they're meatless.

1 cup almonds or walnuts, toasted

2 cloves garlic

2 tablespoons dried parsley

¼ teaspoon kosher salt

Black pepper

1 cup shredded Parmesan cheese, plus more for serving

1 cup panko breadcrumbs

2 large eggs

28 ounces (about 3 cups) marinara sauce of your choice

Flavorless oil, for frying

8 ounces spaghetti, cooked according to package directions

Chopped fresh flat-leaf parsley or basil, for serving

In a food processor, combine the nuts and garlic and pulse to a coarse crumb. Add the parsley, salt, a few turns of pepper, Parmesan, and breadcrumbs and pulse to combine. Add the eggs and process until the mixture holds together in a ball. It may still look crumbly, but it should hold together when you squeeze it. Roll 1½ tablespoon-size balls, packing them just firmly enough so that they hold together but not too firmly because otherwise they'll be tough. Place them on a plate or sheet of parchment paper.

Warm the marinara sauce in a large saucepan over medium heat.

In a skillet, heat ¼ inch of oil over medium-high heat. Working in batches, cook the balls, turning them, until they're golden brown on all sides. (Alternatively, you can deep-fry the suckers if that's what you're into.)

Transfer the balls to the tomato sauce and enjoy over spaghetti, topped with additional cheese and chopped fresh parsley or basil.

This is a delicious all-purpose sauce that transforms vegetables, pastas, and salads into a dish that is **WOWEE-ZOWEE GOOD**

MAGIC SESAME sauce

roasted brussels sprouts

¾ lb brussels sprouts, roasted to a crisp!

toss with magic sesame sauce and enjoy!

≈COMBINE≈

1 tb sesame oil
2 tb honey
3 tb tahini
3 tb soy sauce
2 cloves garlic, smashed
a pinch of crushed red pepper

sesame noodles

½ lb pasta or spiralized cucumbers

Toss with magic sesame sauce, top with chopped scallion and enjoy!

Here are two of my **FAVORITE** applications

Turn Page ↵

FALAFEL FATTOUSH

Makes 4 to 6 servings

At school, the percussionists often observed Waffle Shirt Wednesday, Food Stand Friday, and happy hour every day at Harry's Burritos with Travis the chillest bartender in Manhattan. The percussionists were creatures of habit, which sometimes frustrated me when I'd want to try new cool restaurants downtown and all they'd want to do was go to Chipotle; but it also comforted me when I knew that I could go to Harry's any day at 4 p.m. and find Hammer and Kyle chain-smoking and drinking pre–studio class margaritas.

Food Stand Friday came about because of the really tasty lunch cart that parked on the corner right outside of Juilliard. The guys would usually get a pile of meat on rice and I'd go for the very coriander-y falafel with white sauce and a little tiny bit of hot sauce. An extra-crispy crust and the heavy hand on the coriander separated this falafel from the refined dainty herby balls that I later discovered downtown, but it's probably a draw for which falafel in the world is my favorite. As long as it's salty and crispy and not at all soggy, it pretty much has my vote.

Here, instead of stuffing falafel in a pita or serving over rice, I've counteracted the fried-ness with a bed of fresh vegetables, lemony sumac dressing, and squishy pita croutons. It's not a traditional fattoush, but it's a good one.

Salad

Olive oil or flavorless oil, for frying

3 day-old pitas, chopped or ripped into 1- to 2-inch pieces

Kosher salt

6 lightly packed cups spinach

½ English cucumber or 3 Persian cucumbers, thinly sliced

2 medium tomatoes, cut into ¾-inch pieces

½ small red onion, thinly sliced

2 radishes, thinly sliced

½ cup fresh mint leaves, chopped

Black pepper

Dressing

¼ cup tahini

¼ cup water

1 tablespoon lemon juice

2 cloves garlic, minced

¾ teaspoon sumac

¼ teaspoon kosher salt

Falafel (recipe follows)

To make the salad: In a skillet, heat ¼ inch of oil over medium-high heat until shimmering. Fry the pita pieces until lightly browned, 30 to 60 seconds on each side. Transfer to a paper towel and immediately sprinkle lightly with salt.

(recipe continues)

In a large bowl, combine the pita chips with the spinach, cucumber, tomatoes, onion, radishes, and mint leaves. Season with a few turns of black pepper and salt to taste.

To make the dressing: In a bowl, whisk together the tahini, water, lemon juice, garlic, sumac, and salt, stirring until thickened.

Drizzle half of the dressing over the salad, toss, top with the falafel, and serve with the remaining dressing.

FALAFEL

Makes 14 falafel balls

1 tablespoon coriander seeds

2 teaspoons cumin seeds

1 cup dried chickpeas, soaked for 10 hours or overnight and drained

1 small onion, coarsely chopped

4 cloves garlic, minced

1/4 cup lightly packed cilantro leaves with stems, roughly chopped

1/4 cup lightly packed flat-leaf parsley leaves with stems, roughly chopped

1/4 teaspoon baking soda

1/2 teaspoon ground cinnamon

1 teaspoon kosher salt

Black pepper

A pinch of crushed red pepper

2 tablespoons flour

1 1/2 tablespoons lemon juice

Olive oil or flavorless oil, for frying

Toast the coriander seeds and cumin seeds in a skillet over medium heat until lightly browned and fragrant, then coarsely grind in a spice grinder.

In a food processor, combine the cumin, coriander, soaked chickpeas, onion, garlic, cilantro, parsley, baking soda, cinnamon, salt, a few turns of black pepper, the crushed red pepper, flour, and lemon juice and pulse quickly, 80 to 100 times, until the mixture is combined, but still slightly grainy.

In a large skillet, heat 1/4 inch oil over medium-high heat until shimmering but not smoking. Fry a 1-tablespoon test patty until golden and then taste it. Adjust the seasonings in the mixture as desired. Form balls of falafel mixture, 3 tablespoons each, packing them firmly and then flattening them slightly. Fry on all sides until golden brown. Transfer to a paper towel.

FARM LUNCH

I don't know who I'm kidding here. Farm lunch doesn't look like this. This is the styled staged farm lunch of my dreams inspired by the school lunches of my past and a long-held obsession with cute meals that come separated into individual wrappers and compartments. I've always forced myself to stay awake for the meals on airplanes and hoarded those little jars of condiments that come with room service. When I was young I approached packed lunches in the same way I approached Legos or any other toy. I'd wrap up a crustless baloney sandwich, put Goldfish crackers and Chips Ahoy cookies in a Hello Kitty container, add an Easter egg, and then place it all neatly in a brown paper bag with a pink lemonade juice box, crawl inside of my jungle gym, and then have a picnic. And I'd obviously bring my Molly Doll because she had a great paper bag lunch.

In college I often kept a fridge stocked with mini containers of hummus, individual bags of carrots, hard-boiled eggs, and those cute as a button Babybel cheeses and each morning I'd wrap up one of each in a cloth satchel. Lunch is so fun.

I mourned cute packed lunches when I started working from home, but rejoiced when I learned that part of the responsibility of a farm wife is getting to pack farm lunch! The rules are simple:

• Containers have to be sturdy enough to get tossed around the inside of a tractor.

• Food should be able to be eaten with one hand.

• There should be A LOT OF FOOD.

And for a while in the beginning . . . .

• It should all be gluten-free and dairy-free.

Ugh, no sandwiches. COME ON, EGGBOY. I tried for a little while, putting homemade hummus into brightly colored containers and whole cucumbers wrapped with handwritten notes into small parcels for Eggboy to carry to the farm. I was really proud of myself for thinking up creative ways to make a gluten-free, dairy-free lunch! Until I became privy to the fact that Eggmom was also packing him massive manly lunches that were more appropriate for a farmer working 17-hour days. Big duffel bags filled with beans, steel-cut oats, and nuts upon nuts. It dawned on me that I had no idea how to pack a true farm lunch. They were being so nice to me though, letting me have my cute lunch fun; but in reality, farm lunch isn't meant to be small or cute. And besides, they explained, Egggrandma made most of Eggpop's lunches all the way up until Eggmom retired. So in reality, I had some time before I had to start packing up nondescript bags of unsalted beans since Eggmom already had it under control.

¯_(ツ)_/¯ What are ya gonna do.

In conclusion, two things: 1. Eggmom is a hero of farm lunch, and 2. The farm lunch pictured here is basically just a training session for my future as a Bento mom.

CUTE LITTLE LUNCH

Makes 1 serving

What can be said about the glory of Lunchables that hasn't already been said by every American child under the age of 10?

That these are the greatest lunchies ever made and please can I eat one every day?

That I wish everything in life could be this cute, straightforward, and lovable?

That all of the health activists on Twitter who say mean things to me when I express my undying love for lunchmeat and individual plastic compartments are poo heads with no respect for nostalgia?

Well, I'll show you!

I made a Lunchable from scratch. I spent 10 days in Israel with my Baloney Guru, Culinary Bro-Down's own Josh Scherer, talking about the intricacies and complications of homemade lunchmeat and then I came home, ordered a metal Bento box on the Internet, and made a homemade Lunchable mostly to say that I could. It includes a homemade version of Ritz buttery crackers and homemade Oreos, but I drew the line at cheese since cheddar takes days to make and a bunch of fancy ingredients I'd only be able to get online. If you're looking for a fun weekend project that yields a childhood treat free of preservatives, this is for you!

6 slices Homemade Baloney (recipe below)

6 Buttery Crackers (recipe follows)

6 slices cheddar cheese

6 Lindsay Lohan Cookies (recipe follows)

HOMEMADE BALONEY

Makes 1 pound

1 pound ground beef (80% lean)

2 teaspoons dried onion

2 teaspoons sweet paprika

2 teaspoons kosher salt

4 cloves garlic, smashed

Black pepper

¼ cup ice chips

Coat a plate or baking sheet with cooking spray and spread the beef out in about 1-inch crumbles. Freeze for 20 minutes.

(recipe continues)

In a food processor, combine the beef, onion, paprika, salt, garlic, and a few turns of black pepper and blend continuously for 4 minutes. Continue to blend and gradually add the ice chips over the course of 1 minute.

Divide the mixture in half and either stuff it into 2-inch-diameter sausage casings or mold each half into 2-inch-diameter logs and wrap firmly with plastic wrap, tying the ends with string. (Warning: If you take the plastic wrap route, your baloney will look *extremely* unappetizing until you slice it. Those with sensitive gag reflexes are advised to proceed with caution.)

Freeze for another 20 minutes. Set a large pot of water over high heat to come to a boil.

Reduce the pot of water to a low boil and boil the baloney links for 20 minutes, until they have an internal temperature of 160°F. Transfer them to an ice bath for 5 minutes. Cool in the fridge, slice, and enjoy.

BUTTERY CRACKERS

Makes 20 crackers

1 cup flour, plus more for dusting
½ teaspoon kosher salt
1 teaspoon baking powder
1 tablespoon sugar

¼ cup cold unsalted butter, cut into cubes
⅓ cup cold water

Preheat the oven to 350°F. Line a baking sheet with parchment paper.

In a food processor, combine the flour, salt, baking powder, and sugar and pulse to combine. Sprinkle in the butter and pulse until it's pea-size. Continue pulsing and drizzle in the water until the mixture comes together and forms a ball. Pour onto a work surface and roll out the dough until it is ¼ inch thick, dusting it with flour if necessary. Cut out 2-inch rounds, re-rolling scraps. Transfer them to the baking sheets, ½ inch apart. (Using a small offset spatula helps with this step.)

Bake until lightly browned. Begin checking for doneness at 20 minutes. Let cool on the pan and enjoy. Store in an airtight container at room temperature.

(recipe continues)

LINDSAY LOHAN COOKIES (AKA PEANUT BUTTER SANDWICH COOKIES)

Makes 18 cookies

Come on, put on your worst best British accent and say it with me now,

"I love Oreos. At home, I eat them with . . . I eat them with peanut butter."

And now in a higher-pitched California voice,

"You do?! That is so weird! So do I!"

Okay, you passed, go pierce your own ears. (No, DON'T.)

Cookies

2 cups flour

1 cup unsweetened cocoa powder, plus more for dusting

¾ teaspoon kosher salt

1¼ cups unsalted butter, at room temperature

¾ cup sugar

1 teaspoon vanilla extract

Powdered sugar, for dusting

Filling

½ cup unsalted butter, at room temperature

¼ cup unsweetened smooth peanut butter

1½ cups powdered sugar

1 teaspoon vanilla extract

A pinch of kosher salt (omit if peanut butter is salted)

To make the cookies: Preheat the oven to 325°F. Line two baking sheets with parchment paper.

In a small bowl, whisk together the flour, cocoa powder, and salt. In a stand mixer fitted with a paddle attachment, cream together the butter and sugar until light and fluffy. Mix in the vanilla extract. With the mixer running on low speed, add the flour mixture and beat until just combined. It will still be a bit crumbly. Pour the mixture onto a work surface and give it a few kneads to bring it all together. Wrap half of it with plastic wrap and place it in the refrigerator.

Lightly dust your surface and the top of the dough with a 1:1 mixture of cocoa powder and powdered sugar. Working swiftly and carefully, roll out the dough to ¼- to ½-inch thickness and cut out 2-inch rounds. Transfer them to the baking sheets, 1 inch apart (using a small offset spatula helps with this step). Re-roll the scraps and cut out more rounds. Repeat with the remaining half of the dough.

Bake the cookies until the tops are no longer shiny, about 20 minutes. Cool on the pan for 5 minutes, then remove to a wire rack to cool completely.

To make the filling: With a stand mixer fitted with a paddle attachment, beat the butter and peanut butter until creamy. Gradually add the powdered sugar and beat to combine. Beat in the vanilla and salt.

To assemble, place half of the cookies on a plate or work surface. Pipe a blob of filling (about 2 teaspoons) onto the tops of each of these cookies and then place another cookie on top, pressing slightly.

Refrigerate for a few minutes to allow the filling to firm up. Enjoy! Store in an airtight container in the refrigerator.

BLACK SESAME MILK

Makes about 4 cups

Milk by itself serves really only two main purposes when you're 6. The first is that it holds bubbles really well so if you ever want to have a bubble blowing party with the cool change-color Disney Princess crazy straws that you got from Disney On Ice, using milk is a good way to ensure that the bubbles will overflow out of your cup and maintain their bubbly state until they're halfway across the table. The second primary purpose of milk was a way of softening Oreos to get them the consistency of soggy cake so that you could essentially swallow them whole. The leftover milk was like a thinner, less sweet milkshake and by the time it had served its Oreo-soaking purpose it was usually room temperature. Which was gross. And unfortunate because Oreo-flavored milk sounds like it could have so much potential.

Well never fear, this black sesame milk tastes exactly like that, with some added sweetness and the fancy bonus of a bit of toastiness from the seeds. It is my favorite of the dairy-free milks, even if you need floss on hand in case the seeds get stuck in your teeth.

1 cup toasted black sesame seeds (see Note), soaked for 4 hours or overnight and drained

4 cups cold water

¼ cup honey or maple syrup

1 teaspoon vanilla extract

1 teaspoon almond extract

A good pinch of kosher salt

(recipe continues)

In a high-powered blender, combine the soaked black sesame seeds, water, honey or syrup, vanilla, almond extract, and salt and blend on high speed until very smooth, 2 to 3 minutes. Taste and make any adjustments you'd like. Either enjoy it immediately or strain it to get rid of the crushed sesame seeds. (An easy way to do this is to set a sieve lined with cheesecloth over a container or use a nut milk bag, then slowly pour the mixture through. I like unstrained sesame milk because the granules remind me of the stuff that's left in the bottom of a glass of milk after you've dunked a bunch of Oreos in it. But if you definitely would like to strain it, recycle the leftover crushed sesame seeds in oatmeal, cookie dough, cake, frosting, ice cream, anything you'd like.)

Store the sesame milk in an airtight container in the refrigerator for up to 3 days. You can also freeze it for up to 3 months. Shake well before using.

Note: I buy black sesame seeds in bulk at the Asian grocery store and I like buying them pretoasted because when you toast them yourself, it is super hard to tell if you're burning them, since they're already black.

CAMP

When I turned 12, I began spending my summers zip-lining, climbing up rock walls, and trying to start food fights at Camp Chi, a Jewish camp outside of the Wisconsin Dells that was the apple of every Chicago Jewish kid's eye. We spent our days lounging by the pool and writing letters on Little Twin Stars stationery, and our nights sneaking out to go write odd things in shaving cream all over the boys' cabins. On Friday evenings, the girls would pack in front of the mirror to crimp their hair and get body glittered up for Shabbat services in the outdoor amphitheater. I was so bored during those services. Unlike most of my friends, I convinced my mom early on that Sunday school was not for me, and when it came time for full-on Hebrew school, she didn't even try to disrupt a schedule packed with ice skating and soccer. So I had no idea what was going on, and all I could think about was the fluffy braided challah that I'd soon devour.

"If you don't eat the crust, that's less calories," preached my best friend Gigi from behind a mountain of challah crust as we shoveled the doughy innards into our mouths. We were just beginning to navigate our first year at camp, which included a dating scene of two eligible, mature-for-their-age, sixth-grade bachelors (who were probably named Joshua) versus the entire sixth-grade girl population. Naturally we were all set on being the prettiest tweens we could possibly be; losing our miniature 12-year-old paunches by way of crustless challah was a crucial first step.

By Tuesday's lunch, all bets were off, though, because Tuesday was grilled cheese and tomato soup day, and Camp Chi's grilled cheese was everything that I desired and more. Par-melted American cheese between two slices of barely toasted but heavily buttered white bread, cut into triangles, and dunked into the thinned down tomato puree that we hastily ladled into Styrofoam soup bowls. The Joshuas could wait, this lunch was an event.

Every day, our meals were eaten at the same long table, which eventually became a stage for after-dinner cheers and the Birkat Hamazon, which we bastardized with raunchy words and accompanying dance moves. But again, if I had actually learned the Hebrew, it might have meant a bit more to me, and I might not have been so quick to shout "I share I share my bra" in the place of *a-sher a-sher ba-ra.* (Alright, I might have.)

On Thursday afternoons we took our turn at the canteen, where we bought frozen Charleston Chews and grape slushies, and for the rest of the week I got my sugar fix via care packages from my family members who after a few years of failed attempts learned that candy could be smuggled in under a pile of tampons. Cow Tales, gummy bears, and the resulting street credit of having successfully snuck in nonkosher candy were absolutely worth the embarrassment of having to open a box of high absorbency tampons in front of the sympathetic mail room counselors.

One year, my other best friend Holly and I supplemented our secret candy stashes with a 25-pound box of rainbow sprinkles that we discovered hiding in the cooking classroom. We ate them by the handful as we bonded over a mutual love for Guster and Jack Johnson, and dreamt up future plans to start a sprinkle company called Ollies. And it was that same year, the summer before eighth grade, when our counselors took us on a field trip to one of Wisconsin Dells' many indoor water parks. We weren't allowed to buy food from the concession stand because it wasn't kosher, but ohmygod those few bites of cheese fries that I scarfed down before I was caught remain some of my favorite bites of food that I've ever had. Not just because they were eaten in secrecy, but also because I was never allowed to have nacho cheese back at home.

The last few days of camp were tragic. Knowing that we would soon have to sleep in our bedrooms at home, all alone with no one to gossip with, cast a shadow on the whole camp. We savored those last few days and attempted to break as many rules as possible, sneaking out at night to the tennis courts, and sleeping in as late as we pleased.

What softened the blow of having to say goodbye to all of my camp friends and counselors was knowing that I would soon see my family, live once again in a climate-controlled situation, and most important, get to make up for any lost challah crust calories with my mom's homemade macaroni and cheese, which was ready and waiting for me when I returned.

Her macaroni and cheese is, with the help of Martha Stewart, the best macaroni and cheese in the world. It's a magical creamy mix of Gruyère, cheddar or Swiss, and Parmesan that coats extra-soft macaroni noodles beneath a thick bed of crispy breadcrumbs. There are always leftovers, which were important for getting through those first few days home from camp, and it lends itself well to delicious variations, which I'll never stop experimenting with.

GRUYÈRE MAC AND CHEESE
WITH CARAMELIZED ONIONS

Makes 4 to 6 servings

In my opinion, one of the only things that can make a perfect thing better is dumping in a bunch of caramelized onions. So I did just that with a version of my mom's mac and cheese, and then added some mustard for a tiny zing.

6 tablespoons unsalted butter

1 large onion, thinly sliced

Kosher salt

8 ounces medium shells

¼ cup flour

2½ cups whole milk

6 ounces Gruyère cheese, shredded

4 ounces Swiss cheese, shredded

2 ounces Parmesan cheese, grated

1 teaspoon sweet paprika

¼ cayenne pepper

¼ teaspoon ground nutmeg

2 teaspoons Dijon mustard

Black pepper

½ cup panko breadcrumbs

Preheat the oven to 375°F. Grease an 8 x 8-inch baking dish.

In a large skillet, melt 2 tablespoons of the butter over medium heat. Add the onion and a pinch of salt and cook, stirring occasionally, until browned and caramelized, about 40 minutes.

Cook the pasta according to the package directions, reducing the cooking time by 1 minute. Drain and set aside.

In a large pot, melt the remaining 4 tablespoons butter over medium-high heat. Add the flour, whisking until combined, then cook for 1 minute. Add half the milk, whisking continuously until thickened, about 5 minutes, and then repeat with the other half of the milk. Add the Gruyère and Swiss and all but 2 tablespoons of the Parmesan and stir until the cheeses melt. Stir in the paprika, cayenne, nutmeg, mustard, and black pepper and salt to taste. Stir in the pasta and onions.

Transfer the mixture to the baking dish and top with the panko, a pinch of salt, a few turns of pepper, and the reserved Parmesan and bake until the top is browned, about 25 minutes. Cool for 5 minutes and enjoy.

Note: In a pinch, you can skip the baking step. Simply cook the pasta fully before stirring it into the cheese sauce, then serve immediately topped with panko and Parmesan.

ng," the first dish that my friends specifically
and the one that I had memorized really well in the event that it
needed to be busted out after a long night of Jameson shots. Everyone needs at least
one of those recipes, even if it's just a really good toast. Other people associating you
with nourishment and tastiness rather than puke all over their floor is your primary
goal in college.

This recipe follows the same framework as my mom's mac and cheese, but the Gruyère
and Swiss have been subbed out for smoked Gouda and pepper Jack to give it some sass.
To further the smokiness, bacon fat is used instead of butter in the roux. I thought I was a
mega food genius when I came up with that. Head-to-toe bacon! Or something.

8 ounces medium shells

12 ounces applewood-smoked bacon

¼ cup flour

2½ cups whole milk

¾ pound smoked Gouda cheese, chopped

¼ pound pepper Jack cheese, chopped

1 ounce Parmesan cheese, grated

1¼ teaspoons sweet paprika

½ teaspoon cayenne pepper

¼ teaspoon ground nutmeg

Kosher salt and black pepper

½ cup panko breadcrumbs

Ketchup, for serving

Preheat the oven to 375°F. Grease an 8 x 8-inch baking dish.

Cook the pasta according to the package directions, reducing the cooking time by
1 minute. Drain and set aside.

In a large pan, cook the bacon until crispy. Chop the bacon and set aside. Pour off all
but ¼ cup of the fat in the pan. Heat it over medium-high heat and add the flour,
whisking until combined, and then cook for 1 minute. Add half the milk, whisking
continuously until thickened, about 5 minutes and then repeat with the other half of
the milk. Add the Gouda, pepper Jack, and all but 2 tablespoons of the Parmesan and
stir until the cheese melts. Stir in the paprika, cayenne, nutmeg, and salt and black
pepper to taste.

Fold in the shells and bacon and transfer to the greased baking dish. Top with the
panko, a pinch of salt, a few turns of pepper, and the reserved 2 tablespoons Parmesan.
Bake until the top is browned, about 25 minutes. Cool for 5 minutes and enjoy with
ketchup, if desired.

W~~A~~
WIT~~H~~

Makes 4 to 6 servings

One of the first food writing as~~sig~~.
magazine *The Violet*, which was a beaut~~y~~
over the country. I was given free rein to create fou~~r~~ ~~dishes~~ ~~of mac~~aroni and
cheese of my choosing, and raided the entire cheese section of a Whole Foods in
preparation. In my tiny kitchen I made dish after dish of mac and cheese and invited all of
my percussionist friends to come over and fill out blind-tasting forms so that they could
tell me what to tweak. I attempted an Indian-spiced one that was heavy on the curry
powder, a healthy one with washed rind cheese and spinach (it was gross), and a clear
winner with this Brie baby right here. The Brie melts down so smoothly and the walnut
crust makes it feel fancy enough to bring to wine night with your grownup friends.

8 ounces pipe rigate or medium shells

3 tablespoons unsalted butter

1/2 small onion, finely chopped

Kosher salt

1/4 teaspoon sweet paprika

1/4 teaspoon cayenne pepper

1/4 teaspoon ground nutmeg

1/8 teaspoon ground allspice

Black pepper

1/4 cup flour

3 cups whole milk

1/4 pound Brie cheese, rind removed
and finely chopped

1/4 pound Gruyère cheese, shredded

3 ounces pancetta, cooked and chopped
into 1/2-inch pieces

1 large Granny Smith apple, chopped into
1/2-inch pieces

1/2 cup walnuts, toasted and coarsely
chopped

3 tablespoons shredded Parmesan cheese

Preheat the oven to 375°F. Grease an 8 x 8-inch baking dish.

Cook the pasta according to the package directions, reducing the cooking time by
1 minute. Drain and set aside.

In a large saucepan, melt the butter over medium heat. Add the onion and a pinch of
salt. Cook, stirring, until the onion is soft and translucent, 5 to 7 minutes. Stir in the
paprika, cayenne, nutmeg, allspice, and a few turns of pepper and cook for 2 minutes
more. Increase the heat to medium-high and add the flour, whisking until combined,
then cook for 1 minute. Add half the milk, whisking continuously until thickened,

I HAVE SNACKS

and wine and will do what it takes to have REALLY good Mac at some point tonight

PREHEAT oven to 375°

ALL OF IT

I just ate 7 tacos and can easily wait for a day or 2 before eating again

COOK
½ pound of pasta according to directions on the box BUT REDUCE COOKING TIME BY 1 MINUTE

FANTASTIC

ARE YOU A VEGETARIAN?

YES   NO

CRISP some chopped bacon, pancetta or other fatty meat. Transfer to a plate, and reserve ¼ C of fat HEAT the fat in a large pan.

COMBINE Pour cheese, pasta & meat (if using) INTO 8×8 BAKING DISH

MAKE your pasta and cheese, by FOLLOWING THE PINK ARROWS put in a baking dish, but DON'T BAKE

mix in **¼ C FLOUR** and cook for **1 MINUTE**

Cover with bread crumbs bake for 25 minutes, and **ENJOY!**

ADD CHEESE
ABOUT 12 oz SHREDDED MORE OR LESS IF YOU'D LIKE

WHISK
in 1½ C milk until thickened. ADD 1 MORE CUP OF MILK and whisk until thickened.

REFRIGERATE for 4 HOURS or overnight

STIR
until melted. Add any other seasonings you'd like!

harissa? paprika? cayenne?

CUT INTO CUBES
COAT in:
FLOUR   BEATEN EGGS   BREAD CRUMBS

THEN **DEEP FRY THEM** COVER THEM IN A **TSUNAMI** OF KETCHUP because **YOU ONLY LIVE ONCE**

THE TOKEN GREEN SALAD

Makes 4 servings

"How can something so awful be so healthy?" is what I ask myself almost every time I choke down a bowl of green leafy vegetables. Granted, we don't really have access to good lookin' greens for most of the year, so on a texture scale, our fresh spinach is usually at level: leather. But a green leafy salad, in general, is only something I eat because of that Blue Zones book that says we'll live a little longer if we eat green vegetables. So just like my mom hides meds for the doggies in a little ball of cheese, I like hiding my greens under a big thick layer of bacon and croutons and then giving them a bath in honey and mustard.

This is a main dish salad that's perfect as a lunch or weeknight meal. It'll fill you up, satisfy your salty crunchy cravings, *and* make you feel like you're adding a few more days onto your life (or at least counteracting the days you're subtracting with all that bacon).

8 ounces mixed greens

½ small red onion, thinly sliced

2 cups fresh 1-inch croutons (see Note), seasoned with salt and pepper

12 thick slices bacon, cooked until crisp and chopped into 1-inch pieces

2 avocados, cut into ½-inch pieces and seasoned with salt and pepper

4 large 7-minute eggs, halved lengthwise and seasoned with salt and pepper

Freshly shaved Parmesan cheese

Dressing

½ cup extra virgin olive oil

¼ cup Dijon mustard

2 tablespoons honey

2 tablespoons white wine vinegar

2 cloves garlic, smashed

Kosher salt and black pepper

In a large serving bowl, layer the greens, onion, croutons, bacon, avocados, eggs, and Parmesan.

To make the dressing: In a small bowl or measuring cup, whisk together the olive oil, mustard, honey, vinegar, and garlic. Season with salt and pepper and then dress the salad as desired.

Note: I like making my croutons by cubing up day-old multigrain or challah bread and toasting them on the stove in a layer of butter or olive oil until the outsides are golden and crunchy but the insides are still a bit soft.

SPÄTZLE WITH BRUSSELS SPROUTS AND BACON

Makes 4 servings

Around the time that I was beginning to take percussion seriously, my dad made a comment that was something to the effect of "You can't play a Mahler symphony without knowing German!" referring to all of the sections marked *langsamer* ("slower") and *Schwammschlägeln* ("use soft mallets"). And the thing you must know about every teenage kid who has just fallen in deep with classical music is that *they love Mahler*. Everyone loves Mahler. But teenagers especially because when you're young and hormonal and learning about emotions for the very first time, it's natural to find that only very loud, very intensely passionate Mahler symphonies will satisfy your needs for ***feelings***. You want to shout about the hammer blows in Mahler 6, and cry over fleeting summer memories dancing barefoot through the Tanglewood fields to the Adagietto in Mahler 5.

In other words, I desperately signed up for high school German class so that I could understand the scribbles all over Mahler's music. It didn't take long for me to fall in love with the enormous compound nouns and umlauts scattered about the language, and shortly thereafter I became just as enamored with the food.

My new favorite foods fit snugly into my childhood dogma of noodles and bread and no vegetables. They had fun names like *Knödel* and *Schnitzel* and could be finished off with gummy bears and Kinder Eggs, all in the name of research.

There were a few summers in high school when I took my new language skills over to Germany, to play music and chill with my dad, who had a similar fascination with the culture. On one occasion he and I went to the Hofbräuhaus in Munich and sat at a long communal table as the Oompa band made their rounds. I ate an obscene amount of *Käsespätzle* that was almost as good as my mom's mac and cheese, and when I was finished I persuaded my dad to let me have a taste of his beer. He obliged, probably knowing what was about to happen, which was that I had one teeny tiny sip that felt like fire going into my brain and down the back of my throat. It was painful and I wanted it to be over from the moment it started. My dad watched me cringe and nodded, knowingly, and he was probably thrilled to see that I hated beer so much. But when the pain died away and all that was left was the faint taste of bread, I was slightly intrigued. Intrigued enough to use my status as a 16-year-old to secretly buy beer souvenirs for all of my friends and smuggle them back in my suitcase.

(recipe continues)

"What do you have in here, Myllo? Books??"

"Yup, Pop. Calculus."

Little baby spätzle dumplings are chewy and rustic and slightly nutmeg-y. Specialized spätzle makers exist, but you can get by with strong arms and a slotted spoon. Once boiled, spätzle are typically fried in butter or oil, but because this dish is heavy on the bacon, we're going to use up the fat to brown these nubbins. One rule I always follow with this is to crisp up extra bacon so that you-know-who can nosh on some while I'm pressing out the spätzle.

1½ cups flour

¼ teaspoon ground nutmeg

Black pepper

½ teaspoon kosher salt, plus more to taste

2 large eggs

½ cup whole milk

12 slices thick-cut bacon

¾ pound Brussels sprouts, shredded

Lemon juice

Hot sauce

In a medium bowl, whisk together the flour, nutmeg, a few turns of black pepper, and ½ teaspoon salt. In a separate bowl, whisk together the eggs and milk. Whisk the milk mixture into the dry ingredients and stir to combine. Cover and refrigerate for 30 minutes.

Bring a large pot of salted water to a boil. Working in batches, press the spätzle dough through a greased spätzle maker or greased slotted spoon (the holes should be on the larger side, ¼ to ½ inch) using a rubber spatula and into the boiling water. Cook until the spätzle float to the top, 2 to 3 minutes, then remove with a slotted spoon and transfer to a medium oiled bowl.

In a large skillet, cook the bacon over medium heat until crispy, about 10 minutes. Transfer the bacon to a paper towel. Pour off all but about ¼ cup of the bacon fat from the pan. Chop the bacon into ½-inch pieces and set aside.

Heat the bacon fat over medium heat and add the Brussels sprouts and a good pinch of salt. Cook, stirring very occasionally, until the Brussels sprouts are browned and tender, 4 to 6 minutes.

Add the spätzle to the skillet and cook, stirring often, over medium-high heat for 3 to 5 minutes to give the spätzle some color and ensure that the Brussels sprouts are tender. Stir in the bacon and finish with more black pepper, a squeeze of lemon juice, and a few shakes of hot sauce. Taste, adjust seasonings as desired, and enjoy.

You Can Bánh Mi That

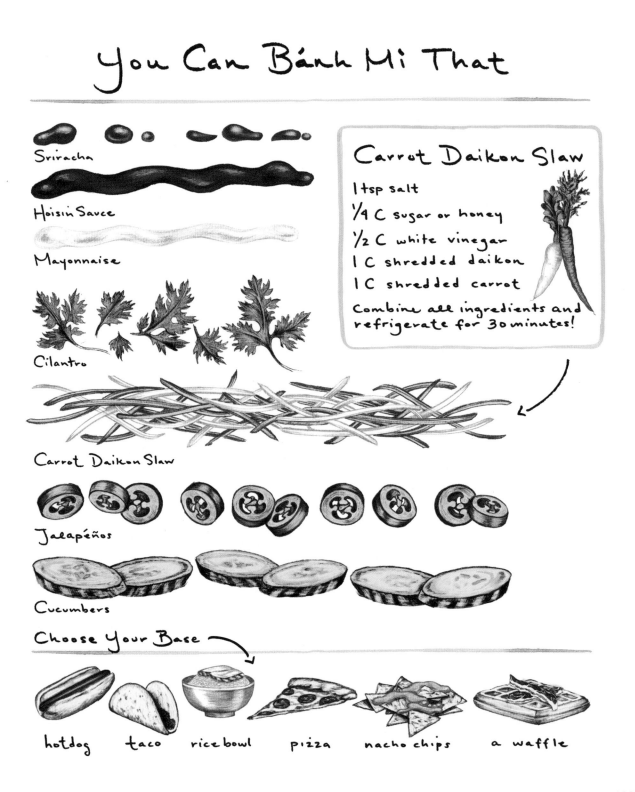

Sriracha

Hoisin Sauce

Mayonnaise

Cilantro

Carrot Daikon Slaw

1 tsp salt
¼ C sugar or honey
½ C white vinegar
1 C shredded daikon
1 C shredded carrot

Combine all ingredients and refrigerate for 30 minutes!

Carrot Daikon Slaw

Jalapeños

Cucumbers

Choose Your Base

hotdog   taco   rice bowl   pizza   nacho chips   a waffle

QUINOA CARBONARA

Makes 2 main-dish or 4 side-dish servings

One great thing that came out of the era when Eggboy was gluten-free was a collection of tasty quinoa recipes. I often subbed out floury things for quinoa and made dishes like quinoa mac and cheese and quinoa pizza casserole. The best remnant from that era, though, was this simple twist on a classic spaghetti carbonara. If you can cook an egg on the sidewalk, and you can cook an egg in a skillet, surely you can cook it with a pile of hot fluffy quinoa.

½ pound bacon, coarsely chopped

1 small onion, finely chopped

2 cups water

½ teaspoon kosher salt

1 cup white quinoa, rinsed and drained

2 large eggs

½ cup grated Parmesan cheese, plus more for serving

Black pepper

In a large saucepan, cook the bacon over medium-high heat, stirring, until browned and crispy. Remove the bacon, keeping the fat in the pan. Add the onion and cook, stirring, until it is soft and translucent, 5 to 7 minutes.

Stir the water, salt, and quinoa into the pot and bring to a boil over medium-high heat. Reduce the heat to medium-low, cover the pot, and simmer until all of the liquid has absorbed into the quinoa, about 20 minutes.

While the quinoa is cooking, in a large bowl, beat together the eggs, Parmesan, and a good few turns of pepper.

Once the quinoa is finished cooking, immediately transfer it to the bowl with the egg mixture and quickly mix it together until the quinoa is evenly coated with the egg. Fold in the bacon, top with additional Parmesan, and serve.

ALL OF THE ALLIUMS FRIED RICE

Makes 4 servings

Alliums are some of the few vegetables that I can truly rely on in the dead of winter, and so I allow them the same love and affection that I give to my summer tomatoes and rhubarb. This recipe is basically how I justify eating a bowl of onions for dinner, and a bit of delicate ginger adds a nice depth of flavor without interfering with the oniony flavor. I recommend using a mix of different alliums here (it's a great way to use up any leftover bits of onion or stray scallions that you have lying around). And ever since a really long time ago when some mayo destined for a katsu spilled onto my fried rice, I've firmly believed that fried rice should be topped with mayo, in addition to Sriracha. Either day-old rice or fresh rice works here (I favor short-grain brown or white rice for its almost mushy chewiness). This is a dish that should be shoveled into your mouth by way of a large bowl and spoon.

2 tablespoons unsalted butter

4 cups finely chopped alliums of your choice: onions, shallots, leeks, scallions, ramps

Kosher salt

Flavorless oil

4 large eggs, beaten

Black pepper

4 cloves garlic, minced

1 tablespoon minced fresh ginger

2 cups cooked brown or white rice

Sriracha and mayonnaise (or Sriracha mayo), for serving

In a large skillet, melt the butter over medium heat. Add the alliums and a good pinch of salt and cook, stirring, until everything is nice and soft and smelling really good, 12 to 15 minutes.

Meanwhile, heat a separate medium skillet over medium-high heat and coat the bottom with a thin layer of oil. When the pan is hot, add the eggs and cook, gently scraping up the bottom with a silicone spatula, until mostly set. Remove the eggs from the heat, season with salt and pepper, give them a rough chop, and set aside. (Alternatively, you could cook the eggs first in the large skillet, then remove them before adding the butter and cooking the alliums.)

Add the garlic and ginger to the alliums and cook, stirring, for 2 more minutes. If the pan looks dry at any time, add a bit more butter or some oil. Add the rice and scrambled eggs and fold to combine. Salt the rice to taste. Increase the heat to medium-high, spread the mixture out evenly over the skillet, and let it cook, uninterrupted, until the bottom is crispy, about 5 minutes. Serve with Sriracha and mayo.

CAULIFLOWER SHAWARMA TACOS

Makes 8 tacos

At least once a week, Eggboy tells me that he wishes he were Mexican. "Why's that?" I ask, playing along like we haven't had the same conversation 100 times before, "So that I could eat tacos every single day!" he exclaims, hinting that we should probably eat tacos real soon, and never minding the obvious fact that he doesn't need to be Mexican in order to eat tacos every day. (His logic is that it would be less weird to eat tacos every day, three meals a day if he was at least a little bit Mexican.)

Maybe he should be Tacoboy.

So while I've yet to take on making *al pastor* or carnitas at home, I have a tendency to drift east towards my comfort zone spices and make *shawarma* for my tacos. Janna Gur's *The Book of New Israeli Food* holds my favorite recipe for at-home chicken shawarma. It uses a perfect blend of garam masala, curry powder, and chicken broth base for a fairly easy way to make you feel like you're hanging on the streets of Israel. I like using a similar approach with roasted cauliflower and the result is delicious. It requires some help in the texture department, so it's important to give the cauliflower enough time in the oven to get crispy, and the sprinkle of chopped raw onions at the end is key for crunch.

¼ cup olive oil

½ teaspoon kosher salt

1 tablespoon garam masala

1 tablespoon curry powder

1½ teaspoons vegetable or chicken broth base

1½ pounds cauliflower florets

1 medium onion

2 tablespoons flavorless oil

8 flour tortillas (6-inch)

Tahini Sauce (page 23), to taste

¼ cup fresh cilantro leaves, finely chopped

Zhoug (optional; page 23), to taste

Preheat the oven to 450°F. Line a baking sheet with parchment paper.

In a large bowl, mix together the olive oil, salt, garam masala, curry powder, and broth base. Add the cauliflower and toss to coat. Spread the cauliflower out onto the baking sheet and bake, stirring occasionally, until browned and crispy, 30 to 40 minutes.

Thinly slice three-quarters of the onion. Dice the remaining one-quarter and set aside for topping. In a skillet, heat the oil over medium-high heat. Add the sliced onion and cook, stirring occasionally, until browned, about 10 minutes.

Warm the tortillas on the stove or in the microwave. To assemble, fill them with cauliflower, fried onion, tahini sauce, raw chopped onion, cilantro, and zhoug (if using).

CHICKEN PAPRIKASH

Makes 4 servings

My ancestors on my mom's side came over from Hungary long enough ago that I grew up assuming they'd always been in New York. Our Hungarian heritage wasn't really something that we talked about that often, unless it was to explain to everyone at the dog park that, yes, our floppy sheep dog pups are supposed to have dreadlocks and their breed is from Hungary. But in recent years, I've become hungrier to learn more about my ancestral homeland, past the pups and the fussy Bartok timpani parts that drove me mad in college, and a thing I've come to majorly appreciate about it is chicken paprikash. In my mind, it serves a similar purpose as mac and cheese: a creamy warming dish that's best eaten with a bowl and spoon from under a pile of blankets on the couch on a cold day. And not only that, but it also requires thinly slicing a buttload of onions, which is one of my favorite ways to relax after a long day, and then cooking them in butter and loads of sweet paprika. It's nature's finest air freshener. My version is easy to make and is a good weeknight meal. I enjoy serving it with day-old sourdough bread, but putting it on top of egg noodles or spätzle (page 106) or mixing in dumplings (page 141) are also worthy options.

2 tablespoons unsalted butter

2 large onions, thinly sliced

Kosher salt and black pepper

2 cloves garlic, minced

2 tablespoons Hungarian sweet paprika

¼ teaspoon cayenne pepper

2 tablespoons flour

1½ cups chicken broth

1 pound boneless, skinless chicken breast or thighs, cut into ¾-inch pieces

¼ cup heavy cream

4 thick slices crusty sourdough bread, toasted, for serving

In a large pot, melt the butter over medium-high heat. Add the onions, a good pinch of salt, and a few turns of pepper. Cook, stirring, until the onions are translucent, 7 to 10 minutes.

Add the garlic, paprika, and cayenne and cook for 2 more minutes, until fragrant. Stir in the flour and then add half of the chicken broth, stirring constantly until it thickens. Stir in the rest of the chicken broth and bring to a boil, stirring often. Reduce to a simmer and add the chicken. Cook, stirring occasionally, until the chicken is no longer pink and cooked through, about 15 minutes.

Stir in the heavy cream, taste, and adjust seasonings as desired.

To serve, divide the paprikash among 4 bowls. Serve with the toasted bread.

PIZZA NIGHT

The sun rises in the morning, it sets at night, and on Fridays we have pizza. No matter the time of year or where we are, we eat some combination of cheese and sauce and bread-like foods on Fridays and it has been this way since the dawn of when my mom decided that after a week of home-cooked dinners, she very rightfully deserved to chill out with wine from a box and a slice of Lou Malnati's.

I've attempted to keep a variety of weekly traditions over the years, such as falafel Mondays or McSorley's Sundays, but the only tradition I've carried with me from the suburbs to New York and then to the farm has been this simple commitment to eat pizza on Fridays. It's my favorite food tradition and one I intend to pass down to generations of future related humans.

There is reason to it. Pizza is obviously really really good, it's easy to find pretty much wherever you are, and the definition of "pizza" can and has been stretched like Silly Putty beyond recognition, making it virtually impossible to get sick of. All of your favorite pizza toppings mixed into a vat of quinoa and then baked until the top is crispy and the innards are gooey? Yeah, that's pizza. Cheese and tomatoes panini-ed between two slices of bread? Sure. Sub out the pizza crust for a bowl of spaghetti? Um, yeah.

We try not to make a habit out of bastardizing the standard definition of pizza, but things happen, like you're at the town pizza parlor where you discover that a secret menu option exists that allows you to order any pizza as nachos instead. Or you realize that you're going over to a friend's house for dinner and they're not yet hip to Pizza Night so you have to pregame with a slice of cheese on toast dipped in ketchup. I'm not proud of this, but it's important because the repercussions of not having pizza on pizza night include forgetting to turn the dishwasher on before bed or accidentally putting a dry-clean-only garment in the dryer the next day. Not having pizza sets an unlucky tone for the weekend ahead.

But I mean, as long as you make some sort of effort, pizza night is pretty forgiving. It's like Halloween: It appeals to all and there's really no pressure beyond the bare minimum. It can be as extravagant as a neighborhood-wide get-together with 30 different toppings and a competition element or as simple as a bite of a midnight slice from the Two Boots on West 95th Street after a long night of drinking and forgetting that it was Friday pizza night. These days, it's often synonymous with date night, and it's when we allow ourselves more TV, more cheese, and another beer.

This constant force of pizza in my life has revealed itself to be more than just a tasty food that's always been there for me, but a barometer for my well-being, for lack of a less dramatic term. Two slices of cheese from Francesco's on 69th Street are more than two perfect greasy specimens of New York pizza, they're signs of my kinda poor but carefree college party nights spent surrounded by percussionist boys whose dating woes I tried to cure with tough love and feedback the way they coached me through my xylophone excerpts during the week. I ate at Francesco's in heels and disco-ready makeup and the guys who worked there knew me by name.

As the years went by, I cruised through New York's Best Pizza lists and collected them all, Pokémon-style. I loved Kesté's chewy crust and the camaraderie built around the samples given to those waiting in the cold for a table; Motorino was a close second and home to pizza nights during my short and sweet vegan phase; and while I never would have admitted this out loud at the time, I'm now far enough removed from it that I can confirm there *is* a time and a place for eating an entire slice of Koronet (which, for the uninitiated, is the size of an average 3-year-old), and that's after eating a pot brownie. I loooooved Donatella Arpaia's glittery gold R2D2 pizza oven and freaked out over the city's first fried pizza. And during one heroic afternoon, I muscled through the severe service flaws at the Upper West Side's short-lived location of Fratelli la Bufala for a really good and almost worth it meaty pizza. A Neapolitan pie meant that I was taking in New York the way that everyone should, hungrily and excited to the point of jazz hands.

So when the newly named Eggboy and I started getting revved up for Domino's delivery to my apartment in Brooklyn, I knew my relationship with New York was going south. It got to a point where I was so enthralled in my homebodiness that on some nights you could have given me a fast pass through the wait at Roberta's and even one of them fancy Ubers there and back and I still would have opted to stay in with Eggboy, Netflix, and two-toppings-medium-pizza-$5.99. The newness of Eggboy was a big part of it, obviously, but that only helped me see that my top requirement for a partner—that they would make a desert island (or a Brooklyn apartment with

Domino's pizza or a farm in the upper Midwest outside the boundaries of restaurant delivery) extraordinarily fun—was filled.

To be clear, we did love Franny's and the other spots around Park Slope and Boerum Hill, but the fact that ordering Domino's in New York wasn't horrifying to me anymore spoke to my weakening commitment to being a New York pizza snob, which is synonymous to being a New York resident.

When I said goodbye to New York, though, I started researching DIY pizza ovens and paying closer attention to things like pizza stones and Jim Lahey. I may have loosened my grip on pizza quality, but I wasn't fully ready to shut down all access to good pizza. For a few rough months before I got my handle on no-knead dough, life in my new town as a pizza eater wasn't fair. During my 1 a.m. shifts at the town bakery, the other bakers would pound leftover rosemary bread dough into rounds and bake it with cheese and *barbecue sauce*. Barbecue sauce! And offer it to me as "pizza." Everywhere else in town, pizza came cut into those Godforsaken squares that haunt me in my sleep. I was open-minded about many things when I moved here, but in the battle of Molly vs. Pizza, I was angry and confused.

What brought me out of it was a mixture of getting intimate with Jim Lahey's no-knead dough, expanding my definition of pizza (such as the aforementioned quinoa casserole and nachos), and recognizing the value in the overall Pizza Night experience. No longer did going out for pizza mean waiting hours for a tiny table in a cramped West Village space, but rather zipping over to Grand Forks' prized pizza parlor, which is named Rhombus Guys and is everything my small-town pizza parlor dreams are made of (as long as you specifically ask for your pizza to be cut into triangles). At home, pizza dough could be made with flour ground from wheat from our farm and vegetables from our garden, and most excitingly, Pizza Night could be had on a tractor.

A NOTE ON PIZZA DOUGH

The only tattoo I've ever seriously considered getting is the ingredients list for Jim Lahey's pizza dough. Somehow I cannot retain it and yet it is the most important recipe, perhaps, ever. The hardest part about making it is allowing it its full resting period of roughly 18 hours, which is why I set an alarm on Thursday nights to start my dough (I highly recommend this). I also highly recommend weighing these ingredients, or at least fluffing the bejeezus out of your flour before measuring it with a measuring cup, in order to ensure a deliciously doughy crust. Here is what my tattoo would be:

2 tsp SALT
500g FLOUR
350g Water
¼ tsp Yeast

    I haven't figured out where it would be, maybe just straight up on the back of my hand. But anyway, this is an extremely condensed version of Jim's recipe (the full one is written in about 1,000 places on the Internet).

    The Recipe: Mix together 500 grams (3¼ cups) flour, ¼ teaspoon active dry yeast, and 2 teaspoons fine sea salt, then stir in 350 grams (1½ cups) water until combined. Cover with plastic wrap and put it down for an 18- to 24-hour nap at room temperature, until it's doubled in sized and bubbling.

HAPPY PIG PIZZA POCKETS

Makes 4 servings

You are correct: Pizza Night does not pause for harvest. It gets even better because it becomes an exciting challenge of "what is the best way to eat a pizza on a tractor?" paired with the uncertainty of whether or not the pizza will be cold by the time an appropriate window of opportunity arrives for me to mount the tractor. (Sometimes I drive out to the field and Eggboy's all the way at the other end loading up a truck and I need to wait a little while until he circles back). Luckily, a pizza is like an escalator in that if it breaks (or becomes cold), it's not out of order, it's just different, and equally good.[1]

The sensation of riding a tractor is a combination of sitting in the front seat of a monorail and riding one of those coin-operated horsey machines. But because you are neither stationary nor attached to a monorail track, there is an element of Mighty Morphin Power Rangers (when they go into their big strong robot machines . . . or is Transformers more relevant to this generation?), so in other words it's pretty awesome, and the fact that pizza is allowed in makes it more awesome.

My favorite time for Pizza Night on the tractor is during wheat harvest because the wheat fields smell like pizza! (The whole experience is like that Alinea course with the pillow that farts a scent pairing to your food. Only it's not actually like that at all because on a tractor you're humble and covered in mud.) And I figured out early on that the easiest way to eat pizza while you're pulling plants out of the ground is in calzone form.

The Happy Pig pizza at Rhombus, the town pizza parlor, is the pizza that made me accept barbecue sauce on my pizza. Because it's really just a pulled pork sandwich that subs pizza crust for the bread. It's littered with the sweetness of pineapple and the crunchiness of peppers and onions, and it's piled with mozzarella cheese as if it's going out of style. In this pizza pocket version, I've swapped out the pulled pork for Canadian bacon (a remnant of growing up with a Jewish-ish mom, when pork was not okay but somehow bacon never counted), and added ricotta to help the filling stay creamy, because without it the fillings glop all to one side.

(recipe continues)

---

[1] *H/T, Mitch Hedburg*

¼ red bell pepper, diced

¼ red onion, diced

2 pepperoncini, chopped

¼ cup chopped pineapple

6 slices Canadian bacon, chopped

½ cup shredded whole-milk mozzarella cheese

¼ cup grated Parmesan cheese

½ cup whole-milk ricotta cheese

2 tablespoons barbecue sauce

A pinch of crushed red pepper

Kosher salt and black pepper

Pizza Dough (page 120)

Flour, for dusting

Preheat the oven with a pizza stone to 500°F. (If you don't have a pizza stone, you can use a baking sheet.)

In a medium bowl, mix together the bell pepper, onion, pepperoncini, pineapple, bacon, mozzarella, Parmesan, ricotta, barbecue sauce, crushed red pepper, a pinch of salt, and a few turns of black pepper.

Divide the pizza dough into 4 equal parts and stretch them into balls. On a lightly floured work surface, flatten them out into rounds about ½-inch thick. Spread each with one-quarter of the filling mixture, leaving a 1-inch border around the edges. Fold them in half to make a calzone shape, pinch the edges to seal, and bake on the pizza stone or hot baking sheet until lightly browned on top, about 10 minutes. Let cool slightly and enjoy.

SQUASH AND RICOTTA PIZZA WITH SAGE AND ARUGULA

Makes two 10-inch pizzas

My first Pizza Night with Eggboy included a really fine squash situation that was complete with homemade ricotta, which we strained through a cheesecloth well past midnight.

Under the dim lights of my kitchen, Eggboy and I caramelized onions and patted out our dough, and we giggled all the way. He took to Friday Pizza Night like a fish to water and I saw this as a very good sign.

2 tablespoons olive oil, plus more for brushing the squash

1 large onion, thinly sliced

Kosher salt

1 teaspoon ground sage

Pizza Dough (page 120)

Flour, for dusting

1 cup whole-milk ricotta cheese

1 cup shaved or grated Parmesan cheese, plus more for serving

Black pepper

4 ounces butternut squash, peeled and shaved with a vegetable peeler

2 cups loosely packed arugula

1½ teaspoons lemon juice

Crushed red pepper, for serving

Preheat the oven with a pizza stone to 500°F. (If you don't have a pizza stone, you can use a baking sheet.)

In a skillet, heat 2 tablespoons of the olive oil over medium heat. Add the onion and a pinch of salt and cook, stirring often, until browned and caramelized, about 30 to 40 minutes. Stir in the sage and cook for 2 more minutes. Remove from the heat.

Divide the pizza dough in half. On a floured pizza peel or baking sheet, flatten out one half of the dough into a 10-inch round. Top with half of the ricotta, half of the Parmesan, a good pinch of salt and a few turns of pepper, half of the onion, and half of the squash shavings. Brush the squash with a thin even layer of olive oil and sprinkle it with salt and pepper.

Bake until the crust and squash are lightly browned. Begin checking for doneness at 8 minutes. Repeat with the other half of the ingredients.

While the pizza is baking, toss the arugula with the lemon juice, a pinch of salt, and a few turns of pepper.

Top the pizzas with the arugula, additional Parmesan shavings, and a sprinkle of crushed red pepper.

ZUCCHINI, WALNUT, AND FRESH MOZZARELLA PIZZA

Makes two 10-inch pizzas

Even though I've mostly figured out my life here re: pizza, I still make it a point to revisit my old favorite pizza places when I go to New York (that is, after I've been to Hummus Place, which is *always* the first stop when I'm in control). I like getting inspired with whatever new toppings they're using and basking in whatever fancy ingredients I wouldn't be able to track down in Grand Forks. Being served an Aperol Spritz with an Italian accent is a plus too.

On one trip in the springtime, I split the tastiest pizza at Don Antonio with my friend Marian, who was sporting her new pink hair and an old floor-length sweater that channeled *Joseph and the Amazing Technicolor Dreamcoat*. The pizza was covered in walnut cream, melty mozzarella, and zucchini and the conversation was centered on her recent solo trip to Disneyland for research on character breakfasts. Everything about it was the kind of whacky shit I need to go back to New York for at least every so often.

But luckily we have walnuts here. The nuttiness on that pizza elevated it from a simple cheesy bread in a way more special than tomato sauce and lighter than pepperoni, so I've since tried to re-create that sensation here. Eventually I moved away from a cream, more toward a walnut pesto, but then ultimately arrived at a garlicky walnut crumble that's all dressed up as sausage. It's even won the heart of Eggboy, who typically prefers about seven different kinds of meat on his pizza.

I like this one in the summer, topped with a squeeze of lemon and washed down with an Aperol Spritz.

1 cup walnuts, toasted

4 cloves garlic

1 teaspoon dried parsley

1 teaspoon dried onion

½ teaspoon anise seeds

¼ teaspoon crushed red pepper, plus more for serving

¼ teaspoon sweet paprika

Kosher salt and black pepper

½ cup shredded Parmesan cheese, plus more for serving

¼ cup olive oil

1 small (6 ounces) or ½ large zucchini, cut into ⅛-inch-thick slices

Pizza Dough (page 120)

Flour, for dusting

½ pound fresh buffalo mozzarella, thinly sliced

Lemon wedges, for serving

(recipe continues)

Preheat the oven with a pizza stone to 500°F. (If you don't have a pizza stone, you can use a baking sheet.)

In a food processor, combine the walnuts, garlic, parsley, onion, anise, crushed red pepper, paprika, ¼ teaspoon salt, and a few turns of black pepper and pulse to a coarse crumb. Add the Parmesan and 2 tablespoons of the olive oil and blend until the mixture clumps together. It might still look crumbly, but it should hold together if you squeeze it in your hand. Taste and adjust seasonings as desired.

In a medium skillet, heat the remaining 2 tablespoons olive oil over medium heat. Add the zucchini and a pinch of salt. Cook, stirring occasionally, until it just begins to brown, about 8 minutes. Transfer the zucchini to a plate lined with a paper towel.

Divide the pizza dough in half. On a floured pizza peel or baking sheet, flatten out one half of the dough into a 10-inch round. Top with half of the mozzarella, half of the zucchini, and dollop on half of the walnut mixture in lightly packed teaspoonfuls (so that it crumbles together to resemble sausage).

Bake until the pizza crust is splotchy with brown marks and the cheese is melted. Begin checking for doneness at 7 minutes. Repeat with the other half of the pizza dough and ingredients.

Finish with a squeeze of fresh lemon juice and additional Parmesan and crushed red pepper.

BUTTER AND SALAMI PIZZA

Makes two 10-inch pizzas

Meet my drug of choice, butter and salami.

When I have no appetite but must eat something so that I don't pass out, butter and salami!

When I barely survived the great breakup of 2010 but had to stand upright at a snare drum, butter and salami!

When the challenge of making new friends in the upper Midwest caused THE MELTDOWN OF THE CENTURY, butter and salami!

I'll never turn down butter and salami, not in the happiest of times, not in the darkest of times. Usually my butter and salami come in sandwich form because that's the easiest. But this one is kicked up a notch on freshly baked pizza dough. Oh slay me it's good. It's basically chicken soup for the soul only it is way more unhealthy than that so if you notice that you start "needing" this pizza more than once a month, maybe it's best to consider other options for your well-being.

Pizza Dough (page 120)

Flour, for dusting

2 tablespoons butter, melted

8 ounces sliced salami, or more if desired

Preheat the oven with a pizza stone to 500°F. (If you don't have a pizza stone, you can use a baking sheet.)

Divide the dough in half. On a floured pizza peel or baking sheet, flatten out one half of the dough into a 10-inch round. Brush it all over with half of the melted butter and then top with half of the salami. Bake until the pizza crust is puffy and splotchy with brown marks and the salami is curly around the edges. Begin checking for doneness at 8 minutes. Repeat with the other half of the pizza dough. Let cool slightly, slice, and enjoy. And then go to the gym.

CELERY DILL SODA

Makes 12 to 16 servings

As much as I wanted to be in that club of people who "grew up with Cel-Ray" or who "is always reminded of their Great Grandpa Larry when they taste Cel-Ray" or who generally have a bunch of happy old-school memories about the celery-flavored soda at their favorite Jewish delis, I'm not because I didn't taste Cel-Ray until well into my twenties as it just wasn't sold around the suburbs of Chicago. It's probably for the better because as a kid who couldn't handle the weird feeling of carbonated beverages, I would have stuck my nose up at it before I could truly appreciate its specialness.

This celery soda is inspired by Cel-Ray, and it's a little ironic because according to deli expert David Sax, many of the first factory workers who made Cel-Ray, at Dr. Brown's, in Brooklyn, were former sugar beet farmers, just like Eggboy, who had emigrated from Eastern Europe. (You learn something new each day!)

And while we're on the subject of Jewish delis, I threw some dill in here because it reminds me of matzo ball soup and because herby sodas are my jam.

½ pound celery, cut into ½-inch pieces

About 12 sprigs fresh dill

2 cups water

1 to 1½ cups sugar

1 teaspoon lemon juice

Carbonated water

First, make a celery-dill simple syrup: In a large pot, combine the celery, dill, and water and bring to a boil. Reduce the heat to low, cover the pot, and simmer for 1 hour. Remove from the heat and strain the celery water into a bowl or large measuring cup (discard the celery and dill).

Measure the amount of celery water (it should be 1 to 1½ cups) and return it to the pot with an equal amount of sugar. Whisk the sugar with the celery water over medium-high heat until the sugar dissolves. Continue to cook until the mixture comes to a boil. Remove from the heat, stir in the lemon juice, and let it cool. This will last for about 2 weeks in the refrigerator.

To make the soda, fill a glass with ice and then add 1 part celery-dill simple syrup to 4 parts carbonated water. Give it a little stir and enjoy.

HARVEST

For the first 23 years of my life, my definition of harvest involved going to the mall and smelling Yankee Candle's harvest-scented votives and then coming home and eating an apple from the grocery store. Sometimes I would talk about my new sweaters with my friends and in Brooklyn, my roommate Patrick threw an annual BYO pumpkin party to celebrate the harvest season with pumpkin carving, mulled wine drinking, and Instagramming in the warm fall light while the smooth sounds of Sufjan Stevens echoed softly through the room.

My cinnamon-scented harvest was romantic and embodied my idea of the farm life in general, which included walking barefoot through crops at sunrise, wearing sundresses, and eating grapes off the vines.

Here's what harvest really is! At least around here.

On our farm, wheat harvest comes first, around early or mid-August. It's a fairly straightforward few weeks of combing through golden fields, collecting dried berries of hard red spring wheat, and bringing them back to the grain bins on our farmstead. Throughout the fall and winter, the grain gets trucked to the North Dakota Mill in town, where it's ground into flour. Wheat should typically be harvested from midmorning until not long after dusk, so while the work days are indeed a bit longer, the chances that Eggboy will be in for supper, or at least a prebedtime episode of *Modern Family,* are high.

Cool. NBD. Wheat harvest, very chill. Smells good, looks good.

The Thing I Usually Kvetch About When I Kvetch About Harvest isn't in reference to Wheat Harvest, though; it's its lunatic monster sister queen, Sugar Beet Harvest. This requires a relentless effort to yank white root vegetables by the ton and bring them immediately to a plant where they're piled into pyramids and cooled down at once, to prevent spoilage. From there they're processed into table sugar, identical to cane sugar.

Because there is such a short timeframe between the time when beets are fully grown and when winter obliterates the area, beet harvest runs for 24 hours a day, 7 days a week, starting October first and going for however long it takes. The 24-hour workdays are broken into two shifts, so technically Eggboy should be either out the door a little before noon and home right after midnight, or vice versa. But as I learned while standing over a pot of shakshuka during my first harvest, this is never the case! Like, ever! *Luckily*, I also learned that holding a pot of shakshuka for 2 hours on the lowest heat setting on the stove makes a damn good shakshuka, but that was a silver lining.

It was during that harvest that I was also working the breakfast pastry shift at the town bakery, which started at 1 a.m. So for a solid bit of time, I'd eat my 11 a.m. supper as Eggboy ate his 11 a.m. breakfast, giving a whole new meaning to breakfast for dinner. That was the only time we'd see each other, since it wasn't uncommon that his 12-hour shift morphed into a 17-hour shift. And because I didn't have any friends yet, that was essentially my unit of human interaction for the day, save for the sleepy hours spent with the two or three other bakers.

This was when we were living in our little almost-windowless apartment in downtown Grand Forks, so my life was a lot like *Cast Away*, but instead of an island and Wilson, I had a kitchen and my blog. So that's pretty much how I became a full-time blogger, by having nothing else to do.

As the years went on, I learned what to expect out of harvest. That it might be as short as 10 days or as long as a month, that I shouldn't make anything for dinner that's time-sensitive, and that I should sign up for a ceramics class or embrace the added alone time with TV shows that Eggboy can't stand. With each new harvest came quirky unexpected side effects, like I discovered a new obsession with hip hop dance tutorials on YouTube or honed my breakfast-in-bed skills when he had the noon shift and didn't wake up until late in the morning.

When the shell shock of my first harvest faded, I came to appreciate how special of a time it is. The farm hires seasonal workers to help drive the trucks and I like to unload my baked goods on them. All around town little chunks of sugar beets lay scattered about the roads as if they have fallen like snow. And in my head, the *Sesame Street* sugar beet song plays on repeat like an October theme.

At night during sugar beet harvest when all is silent except for the hum of the harvesters and the blowing of the wind, you can look out into the horizon to see the twinkling stars and the lights of the tractors against the dark fields. It's as if the sky never ends and the stars go on forever. It's all very romantic. Mud-scented and romantic.

SLOW COOKER GOULASH
WITH SCALLION KNÖDELN

Makes 8 servings

We got married in –13°F, apparently. I don't remember it being that cold, all I remember is the snowfall that arrived just in time for the photos, allowing me to breathe a heavy sigh of relief because one of the main reasons that we had our wedding on the farm in the dead of winter was because we wanted a snowy white wedding. I only hope that all of our guests have forgiven us by now.

While the logical thing to do might have been to take a tropical honeymoon, we jetted off to the Alps for mountains of coziness. We spent 2 weeks having afternoon slices of cake every single day and sipping the best coffee in the world. The only bad part about it was when we tried skiing in the Kitzbühel Alps, at which point I soon found myself sobbing into a mountaintop schnitzel, googling How the Fuck to Ski.

One of the best parts about our honeymoon was the steamy goulash that came with big round *Knödeln* the size of my head. These knödeln were big bready balls of glee that were just like the Wonder Bread balls of my youth but BETTER because they had cheese holding their parts together. They're the perfect way to make a rich dish like goulash even richer. Going into our trip, I knew the schnitzel would be epic, but the biggest takeaway of the trip ended up being my desire to make goulash.

Here is a classic Austrian goulash that you can have simmering away in your slow cooker all day, ready to great you when you come in from the cold.

2 pounds chuck, cut into 1-inch pieces

Kosher salt and black pepper

Flavorless oil, for cooking the beef

1 large onion, chopped

4 carrots, chopped

4 cloves garlic, minced

2 tablespoons sweet paprika

1 tablespoon tomato paste

1 teaspoon caraway seeds

1 teaspoon Worcestershire sauce

2 bay leaves

4 cups vegetable or beef broth

½ cup red wine

1 can or carton (28 ounces) chopped tomatoes

Scallion Knödeln (recipe follows)

Chopped scallions or parsley (optional), for serving

(recipe continues)

Season the beef with ½ teaspoon salt and a few turns of pepper. In a large skillet, heat a thin layer of oil (a few tablespoons) over medium-high heat. Working in batches, brown the meat on all sides, adding more oil to the pan if it dries out. Transfer the beef to a large slow cooker.

Drain off some of the fat from the skillet if needed (you want there to be just a light coating) and add the onion, carrots, and ¼ teaspoon salt. Cook, stirring, until softened, about 10 minutes. Add the garlic, paprika, tomato paste, and caraway seeds and cook for 2 more minutes. Transfer the mixture to the slow cooker along with the Worcestershire sauce, bay leaves, broth, wine, and tomatoes and cook on high for 4 to 6 hours or low for 8 to 10, until the beef is tender.

About 30 minutes before serving the goulash, make the knödeln. To serve, ladle the goulash into bowls and add a knödel. Top with chopped scallions or fresh parsley, if desired.

Note: If you'd like to make this on the stove, use a large Dutch oven or pot and simmer it, covered, for about 2½ hours, or until the meat is tender.

SCALLION KNÖDELN

Makes 8 knödeln

½ cup flour

¼ teaspoon ground nutmeg

¾ teaspoon kosher salt

Black pepper

2 large eggs

½ cup whole milk

12 ounces stale bread, cut or torn into ½-inch cubes

3 scallions, finely chopped

6 ounces Swiss or Gruyère cheese, shredded

In a small bowl, whisk together the flour, nutmeg, salt, and a few turns of pepper. In a large bowl, whisk together the eggs and milk. Add the bread cubes, scallions, and cheese and stir to combine. Mix in the flour mixture and let sit for 15 minutes.

Bring a large pot of salted water to a boil. Using a ⅓-cup ice cream scoop, form firmly packed balls of the mixture and boil them until firm, 15 to 20 minutes.

TOMATO AND SQUASH SOUP

Makes 8 to 10 servings

Harvest could end tomorrow, it could end next week. What's for sure is that once all of the beets are plucked, a big party happens within 24 hours to close out the season and celebrate "another good year." Even if it was a brutal one, it's always "another good year."

For Eggmom and me, it's a drop-everything-and-cook scenario because it's a job we take seriously, cooking for all of the truck drivers and their wives.

Here's a soup that's an Eggmom original. It's a tomato soup thickened with squash puree instead of cream, a remnant from when Eggboy didn't do dairy.

1 butternut squash (2½ to 3 pounds), halved lengthwise and seeded

2½ tablespoons olive oil, plus more for serving

¾ teaspoon kosher salt, plus more to taste

Black pepper

¼ teaspoon ground cinnamon

¼ teaspoon sweet paprika

¼ teaspoon cayenne pepper

⅛ teaspoon ground cloves

1 large onion, chopped

4 cloves garlic, minced

Leaves from 4 sprigs fresh thyme

2 cans (28 ounces each) fire-roasted tomatoes

3 cups vegetable broth

Parmesan cheese, for serving

Preheat the oven to 375°F.

Place the squash halves cut side up on a baking sheet and brush the insides with ½ tablespoon of the olive oil. Sprinkle evenly with ¼ teaspoon salt, a few turns of black pepper, the cinnamon, paprika, cayenne, and cloves and bake until a fork pokes easily into the center. Begin checking for doneness after 1 hour.

Meanwhile, in a large pot, heat the remaining 2 tablespoons olive oil over medium heat. Add the onion and remaining ½ teaspoon salt. Cook, stirring, until the onion is soft and translucent, 5 to 7 minutes. Add the garlic and thyme and cook for 2 more minutes. Transfer the mixture to a blender or food processor, add the tomatoes with their juices, and blend until very smooth. Return the mixture to the pot.

Scoop the insides out of the squash and place it in the blender with the vegetable broth and blend until very smooth. Add it to the pot, bring it to a boil over high heat, then reduce to a simmer. Simmer, covered, for 20 minutes, stirring occasionally. Taste and adjust seasonings as desired. Ladle into bowls, drizzle with olive oil, and top with grated Parmesan.

KNOEPHLA SOUP

Makes 8 to 10 servings

Somewhere in Germany, there is a lucky little Haribo-eating equivalent of my 8-year-old self whose mum makes her *Knoephla* soup every time she is home sick from school. Dumplings are a sick kid's best friend, just like matzo ball soup came to the rescue anytime I was little and home from school.

Knoephla dumplings are like plumper spätzle and they go perfectly in creamy potato soup. They made their way to the upper Midwest with German immigrants, and they've stuck around ever since because they're quite the popular ones.

The town bakery, Dakota Harvest, serves knoephla soup every Tuesday, and every Tuesday it sells out fast. It's creamy and filling but it doesn't have that heaviness that makes you feel like you wanna die after eating it. It's filled with small square dumplings that look like mochi bits before they're boiled; grocery stores around here sell knoephla in the frozen aisle, and they are the cutest little things. The surplus of dumplings and a heavy dose of nutmeg gives a beautiful depth and heartiness to Dakota Harvest's knoephla that helps makes it the best knoephla in all the land. So good that Eggboy and I had them make it for our wedding. Making knoephla is dead simple, especially if you can get your hands on some store-bought dumplings, and it is the food equivalent to burrito-ing yourself in a fluffy blanket.

2 tablespoons unsalted butter

1 large onion, finely chopped

2 large carrots, finely chopped

2 celery stalks, finely chopped

Kosher salt and black pepper

2 cloves garlic, minced

½ teaspoon ground nutmeg

7 cups chicken or vegetable broth

2 bay leaves

1½ pounds red potatoes, cut into ½-inch pieces

2 cups (1 pound) store-bought frozen soup dumplings or homemade Dumplings (recipe follows)

½ cup heavy cream

In a large pot, melt the butter over medium-high heat. Add the onion, carrots, celery, a good pinch of salt, and a few turns of pepper and cook, stirring often, until the vegetables soften slightly, about 10 minutes. Add the garlic and nutmeg and cook, stirring, for 2 more minutes, until fragrant.

Stir in the broth, bay leaves, and potatoes, increase the heat to high, and bring to a boil. If using store-bought frozen dumplings, add them when the soup reaches a boil. (If using homemade dumplings, begin making them when the soup reaches a boil and then add them for the last 10 minutes of simmering.) When the soup reaches a boil, reduce the heat to a simmer, cover, and cook for 30 minutes, stirring occasionally.

Stir in the cream. Taste and adjust seasonings as desired. Remove the bay leaves before serving.

DUMPLINGS

Makes 8 to 10 servings

2 cups flour
1 teaspoon baking powder
¾ teaspoon kosher salt

Black pepper
A pinch of ground nutmeg
¾ cup water

In a medium bowl, whisk together the flour, baking powder, salt, a few turns of pepper, and the nutmeg. Stir in the water and mix to form a shaggy dough. Turn it out onto a clean work surface and knead it for a few minutes, adding flour as needed, until you have a smooth stiff dough. Roll it into ½-inch-thick snakes, cut crosswise into ½-inch pieces, and drop them directly into simmering soup.

NO-KNEAD GARLIC BREAD

Makes 1 loaf

On paper this bread is kinda like that boy who on the surface doesn't really seem dateable because he just swallowed three heads of garlic and requires a 12- to 24-hour rising time, thereby not giving you the instant satisfaction of being a good texter— I mean quickbread. But bear with me here and give this guy some patience, because in reality this is the bread that your soup wants to marry and your parents want to meet. He's got a handsome crust and the deep flavor of a fine aged, um, bread dough.

This thing takes time, but most of it is spent waiting. No kneading or really doing any step that takes longer than 10 minutes at a time. Just a few simple steps over a long period of time will yield a beautiful flavorful loaf.

About 4½ cups bread flour

½ teaspoon active dry yeast

2 teaspoons kosher salt

1⅓ cups warm water

3 heads garlic

About 1 tablespoon olive oil

In a large bowl, combine 3 cups of the flour, the yeast, and salt. Stir in the water until combined. Cover the bowl tightly with plastic wrap and let it rise overnight at room temperature, 12 to 24 hours.

Preheat the oven to 400°F.

Cut the tops off of the garlic heads to expose the tops of the cloves and drizzle about 1 teaspoon of olive oil over the top of each to cover the exposed parts of the cloves. Wrap each head individually in foil and bake until a fork pokes easily into the cloves, about 45 minutes. When they're cool enough to handle, squeeze all of the cloves into a medium bowl and mash them up.

Drop dollops of the garlic over the dough in the bowl and use a spatula to fold it into the dough so that it gets evenly distributed.

Place a large piece of parchment paper on a work surface and lay down a thick layer of flour, ½ to ¾ cup. Scrape the dough onto the floured surface and use heavily floured hands to shape it into a roundish blob. Sprinkle the top with another thick layer of flour, coat a piece of plastic wrap with cooking spray and cover the dough blob. Let it sit on the parchment paper for another 1½ hours.

During the last 30 minutes of sitting time, preheat the oven to 450°F, with a lidded Dutch oven in it. (Make sure your Dutch oven and its lid are heatproof at 450°F.)

Carefully remove the Dutch oven from the oven and remove the lid. Remove the plastic wrap from the dough and use the parchment paper to lift it up and lower it into the Dutch oven (correct, the parchment paper goes in too). Trim any excess edges from the paper (a little overhang is fine) and cover the Dutch oven. Stick it into the oven and bake for 30 minutes, remove the lid and bake until it is nicely browned on top, another 15 to 20 minutes.

Remove it to a wire rack, let it cool for about 30 minutes, and then rip some off and dunk it into a bowl of soup.

HOTDISH

The north wall in our kitchen has a large set of built-in shelves that were custom made in the 1960s for Egggrandma. Until we reworked them to accommodate the sort of bulk grains and nuts that we breeze through on a daily basis, the shelves were very short and very deep and built on a slant so that when one can was removed, another would roll forward in its place.

A handwritten label that designated a shelf for cream of mushroom soup remains and now houses quinoa and Parisian tea.

Growing up, "Is there cream in that?" was my mom's, and later on my, knee-jerk response to any waiter's recitation of the soup of the day. No cream meant that it was acceptable, while a creamed soup didn't stand a chance. In my mom's kitchen, with the exception of tomato, soup was always *always* clear; heavy cream—with its high content of the '90s villain, Fat—was reserved for special-occasion whipped cream.

But as I began my education on traditional foods of the upper Midwest, I soon started to wonder if continuing my family's practice of denying the existence of creamed soup would mean denying Eggboy the comfort food of his childhood: Hotdish.

Hotdish, which is one word, is a subset of the casserole and it's a common thing to bring to a potluck or the house of a friend who has just had a baby. While a casserole can refer to things like macaroni and cheese or creamed corn, a hotdish follows this equation:

Common church cookbook variations include wild rice hotdish (wild rice, chicken or turkey or beef, cream of anything soup, and onions or celery), "Busy Day Hotdish" (ground beef, cream of mushroom soup, onions, and potatoes or frozen french fries), and of course Tater Tot Hotdish (ground beef, cream of anything soup, vegetables, and Tater Tots).

Eggboy's hotdish of choice was Chicken Wild Rice Hotdish.

So one day, a few months before our wedding, I decided to try my hand at being a Midwestern farm wife and went to the SuperTarget, where I bought two cans of Campbell's cream of onion soup. I quickly threw them into my basket and then covered them with a pile of kale. I was so nervous that someone would see me and judge me for going against what my mom had taught me, but Eggboy's reaction would be worth it.

As I unloaded my groceries onto the cream of mushroom soup shelf, my mom's voice whacked me over my head with the line she always used at the grocery store when I wanted to buy processed things. *Don't be silly, we can make that from scratch.*

And with that, visions of béchamel and coconut milk danced before me, whispering softly, "You can do this, Molly. You can make a hotdish." So I set off with my can opener and roux spoon, and I dove head first into the world of hotdish, pleasing the health-conscious Eggparents, the nostalgia-craving Eggboy, and my desire to be a good Midwestern farm wife, all at once. And I'm proud of my results! There's a reason that a big hot bowl of meat, vegetables, starch, and creaminess is so popular up here: It's all you could ever want when it's goddamned fucking –30°F.

CHICKEN POT TOT HOTDISH

Makes 6 to 8 servings

The battle of Most Iconic Hotdish would probably come down to Tater Tot versus wild rice, which is kind of like arguing over which Matthew McConaughey role is the most definitive, *How to Lose a Guy in 10 Days*? Or *Dallas Buyers Club*? This is a test, you're being judged. Before we make fools of ourselves, let's look at this systematically:

• Tater Tot hotdish looks like a Magic Eye picture from a bird's-eye view: +10 points

• Wild rice hotdish looks like poop and snot from a bird's-eye view: −5 points

• Tater Tot hotdish requires you to go out in public and buy premade frozen tots: −5 points

• And using homemade tots kind of misses the point: 0 points

• But it uses tots!!!: +5 points

• Wild rice hotdish features a local Minnesota specialty, widely available at cute local farm stands: +10 points

• Tater Tot hotdish is a little janky: −3 points

• Wild rice hotdish is probably the most sophisticated of the hotdishes: +4 points

• Tater Tot hotdish tastes like childhood: +12 points

• Wild rice hotdish tastes like you're ready for grandkids: +10 points

> Tots: 19 points
> Wild rice: 19 points
> Tie.
>
> I rigged it because the Midwest has softened me on the theme of "Things aren't better than each other, they're just *different*." But that's also pretty much exactly the case with these two champions of northern cuisine. They're different, but equal in comfort and goodness, and perfect on a cold winter day.
>
> Tater Tot hotdish is typically ground beef, creamed soup (often mushroom), some sort of vegetable (probably peas or green beans, maybe some corn), and then, in the words of Sam Sifton,

You cover the bitch with Tater Tots

(recipe continues)

But you don't just throw them on like an abstract topping, you have to let your OCD hang out a little and organize them in rows and columns, as neatly as possible. This organizing of the tots might be one of the most sacred food rituals in the Midwest, second only to making lefse (page 207).

My Tater Tot hotdish has the body of a chicken pot pie, a dish that I loved growing up, long before I knew the existence of Tater Tot hotdish. But a close examination reveals that the only real differences are the subbing of chicken for ground beef and the use of a homemade cream of chicken soup instead of mushroom soup. I don't think this will offend a hotdish purist.

3 tablespoons unsalted butter

1 large onion, finely chopped

3 carrots, cut into 1/2-inch pieces

Kosher salt

6 tablespoons flour

3 cups whole milk

Enough chicken broth base to make 3 cups broth

3/4 cup peas, fresh or frozen

1 1/2 pounds boneless, skinless chicken thigh, cut into 1/2- to 3/4-inch pieces

1/2 teaspoon dried thyme

Black pepper

18 ounces frozen Tater Tots

Ketchup, for serving (optional)

Preheat the oven to 400°F.

In a large skillet, melt the butter over medium-high heat. Add the onion and carrots and a pinch of salt and cook, stirring until soft, about 10 minutes. Stir in the flour so that it gets evenly distributed. Add 1 1/2 cups of the milk, stirring constantly until thickened. Repeat with the remaining 1 1/2 cups milk. Stir in the chicken broth base, peas, chicken, thyme, and a few turns of pepper and simmer, stirring often, until the chicken is cooked through and no longer pink, 10 to 15 minutes. Taste the mixture and adjust seasonings if desired.

Transfer the mixture to an 11 x 8-inch baking dish (or other 3-quart ovenproof dish) and cover the bitch with Tater Tots. Arrange them snugly and neatly. Bake until the tots are golden brown. Begin checking for doneness at 30 minutes. Let cool slightly and serve with ketchup, if desired.

WILD RICE HOTDISH WITH RAS EL HANOUT AND DATES

Makes 6 to 8 servings

And here is my wild rice hotdish, which I am presenting with the hope that the very small intersection of Those Who Use Ras el Hanout on the Reg and Those Who Are Hip to the Hotdish might grow by at least one today.

This hotdish bursts with the flavor of the Moroccan spice mix ras el hanout and gets a nice bit of sweetness from dates and coconut milk, whose richness is balanced by a squeeze of lemon and sprinkle of fresh parsley.

Morocco and the Midwest might be the exact opposite places on earth, but when the flavors of one infuse the dish of another, the result makes you think they're not so far apart. Insert some nice metaphor here for how the world is small, and we should all just get along.

¾ cup wild rice, rinsed and drained

2 cups water

¾ teaspoon kosher salt

5 tablespoons olive oil

1 large onion, finely chopped

4 large carrots, cut into ½-inch pieces

Black pepper

4 teaspoons Ras el Hanout (recipe follows)

1 pound ground beef (85% lean)

¼ cup flour

1 can (13.5 ounces) full-fat coconut milk

1⅓ cups beef or vegetable broth

⅓ cup packed pitted dates, cut into ½-inch pieces

1 sleeve saltines

¼ cup chopped fresh flat-leaf parsley

1 tablespoon lemon juice

Preheat the oven to 375°F. Grease a 13 x 9-inch baking dish. (Alternatively, if you use a Dutch oven to cook the onion mixture—see below—you can bake the mixture in the Dutch oven.)

In a medium saucepan, combine the wild rice, water, and ¼ teaspoon of the salt and bring to a boil over high heat. Reduce the heat to a simmer, cover, and cook for 30 minutes. Drain the rice and set it aside.

In a large pot or 4-quart Dutch oven, heat 4 tablespoons of the olive oil over medium-high heat. Add the onion, carrots, a few turns of black pepper, and ¼ teaspoon of the salt

(recipe continues)

and cook, stirring, until soft, about 10 minutes. Add the ras el hanout and cook for
2 more minutes and then add the beef and remaining ¼ teaspoon salt. Cook, breaking
up the meat with a spoon, until it is no longer pink. Add the flour and stir to combine.
Add the coconut milk and cook, stirring, until thickened, and then add the broth and
cook, stirring, until thickened. Add the dates. Reduce the heat to low and simmer for
10 minutes. Taste and adjust seasonings as desired. Stir in the wild rice and mix to
combine. If not using a Dutch oven, pour the mixture into the baking dish.

Place the saltines in a large zip-top bag, crush them up, then toss them with the
remaining 1 tablespoon olive oil. Spread the crackers over the top of the dish. Bake
uncovered for 35 minutes. Top with fresh parsley and lemon juice. Let cool slightly
before serving.

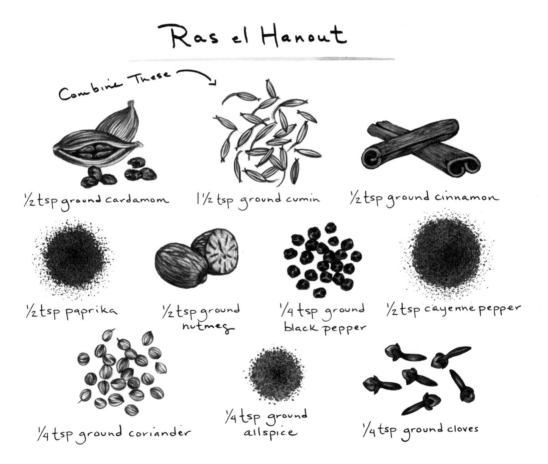

Ras el Hanout

Combine These

½ tsp ground cardamom   1½ tsp ground cumin   ½ tsp ground cinnamon

½ tsp paprika   ½ tsp ground nutmeg   ¼ tsp ground black pepper   ½ tsp cayenne pepper

¼ tsp ground coriander   ¼ tsp ground allspice   ¼ tsp ground cloves

SPRING VEGETABLE AND QUINOA HOTDISH

Makes 6 to 8 servings

Spring here means snowstorms, flooding, and then planting season. Tractors and farmers come out of hibernation and start working more and more hours as the days get longer. It's a transition, for sure, but if you come well equipped with more cookbooks to read, projects to start, and meals that last for a long time in the oven, a husband coming home hours late doesn't seem all that bad. Here's a hotdish for the beginning of spring, when it's still a little chilly but the flavors are ripe for their seasonal debut.

It's a vegetarian hotdish, so it's true that I'm bending the rules a little; but in the absence of meat, quinoa has taken over to make this a hearty nutrient-packed hotdish that's ready for the future, when everyone's vegetarian and gluten-free or whatever.

1¼ cups white quinoa, rinsed and drained	¼ cup flour or gluten-free flour
1¾ cups water	2 cups whole milk
1 bay leaf	1 cup vegetable broth
¾ teaspoon kosher salt	Black pepper
¼ cup unsalted butter	Tabasco sauce
2 large leeks, finely chopped	¼ pound white cheddar cheese, grated
4 scallions or ramps, finely chopped	¾ cup whole-milk ricotta cheese
2 cloves garlic, minced	½ cup peas, fresh or frozen
¼ cup chopped chives	½ cup grated Parmesan cheese
2 cups packed spinach or chopped kale	½ cup panko or gluten-free breadcrumbs

Preheat the oven to 375°F. Grease a casserole dish.

In a medium saucepan, combine the quinoa, water, bay leaf, and ¼ teaspoon of the salt and bring to a boil over high heat. Reduce to a simmer, cover, and cook until all of the liquid is absorbed. Begin checking for doneness at 15 minutes. Discard the bay leaf, fluff the quinoa with a fork, and set aside, covered.

In a large pot, melt the butter over medium-high heat. Add the leeks and ¼ teaspoon of the salt and cook until they begin to soften, about 7 minutes. Add the scallions, garlic, and chives and cook, stirring, for 2 more minutes. Add the spinach or kale and cook, stirring, until wilted. Add the flour and stir to combine. Add the milk and cook, stirring, until thickened, then add the broth and cook, stirring, until thickened.

Reduce the heat to low. Season with a good few turns of black pepper and Tabasco sauce. Add the cheddar, ricotta, peas, and ¼ cup of the Parmesan and stir until the cheese is melted. Taste and adjust seasonings as desired.

Stir in the quinoa, then pour the mixture into the baking dish, spreading it out evenly. Top it with the panko and remaining ¼ cup Parmesan and bake until lightly browned on top. Begin checking for doneness at 30 minutes. Let cool slightly before serving.

III
SNACKS AND CELEBRATIONS

DAILY LIFE ON THE FARM

On most mornings I wake up naturally or to the sound of Tofu's cockadoodle doos resonating from the coop. From bed I check Instagram and Twitter a million thousand times before absorbing a few mugs of undiluted cold brew or Eggboy's blackest black coffee and then I venture off to do any sort of physical activity that will allow me to feel less bad about spending the day baking. On the off chance that it's warm enough to run outside but not so warm that the mosquitos have emerged, I run down the gravel roads surrounded by fields that are so flat you can see farmland to the horizon. But on most days, I do yoga or Pilates or dance videos from the climate-controlled indoors, and wave to Macaroni from the window as Eggboy collects their eggs.

I keep a dry-erase board on the fridge with a list of recipes to develop, photograph, and blog about. Sometimes I think I like developing the best because I get to pull out all my books, sit on the floor, and read everything that's ever been written about bread pudding or scrambled eggs while messaging my circle of friends to discuss schnitzel technique or whether coconut rice *onigiri* would ever be a good idea. Noodling around in the kitchen, finding roux problems to solve and layer cakes to frost is a good way to spend the day.

But then when the storms roll in and the mood in my dining room photo studio is Deliciously Cloudy, I think I like styling and photographing the best. On those days, I could sit at my table all day with tweezers tweaking sprinkles on a cake, debating if it needs a marzipan cow or a squirrel, and eventually getting around to eating a slice, but not before Eggpop knocks on the door asking for 1 cubic inch to test. Word gets around the farm fast when there is cake on the table.

When it's not harvest or planting season, Eggboy usually comes in for lunch at around noon, scopes out the situation to see if there are any recipes he can taste-test for lunch, and sits with the newspaper or fills me in on the goings-on about town. I usually draft him for help with my other favorite part about blogging, writing the thing. Eggboy's humble Midwestness balances out my occasional tendency to word vomit with no filter.

Throughout the day, I correspond with blog readers and check in on the gaggle of Twitter voices swarming the net. From my kitchen on the farm in the middle of nowhere I love that I can see what's happening in the world of babka and keep up with my favorite bands. My other favorite part about blogging is the community and the bonds that I've formed over cakes and photography (okay, sorry, this is getting mushy).

If I'm in need of groceries that aren't things I can pull from the garden or backyard, I journey into town to the East Grand Forks Hugo's or the SuperTarget, which is half an episode of *A Prairie Home Companion* away, and I take my time and peruse what's new. Usually I come away wishing we had a better cheese selection. But it's a small price to pay for life up here.

In the evening when Eggboy comes in from the fields, we cook dinner and pour wine as the chickens find their way into the coop, and the loudest sounds around us are the crackles of the butter as the onions cook.

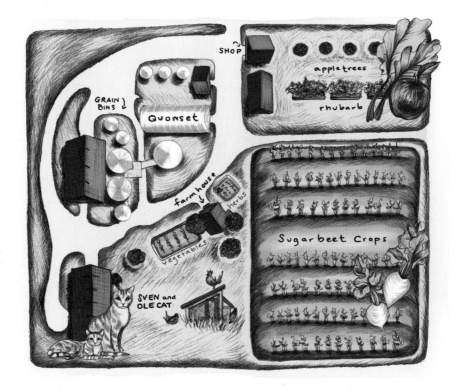

JERUSALEM BAGEL DOGS

Makes 8 large bagel dogs

Second only to the floppy sheepdogs that I grew up with, my favorite breed of dog is the bagel dog. These are inspired by those big oval bagels that you get from street carts in Jerusalem. On the airiness spectrum of bagels, where Montreal is on the left and New York is in the center, Jerusalem bagels are wayyyy on the right. They are so light and cloud-like, and just a little bit chewy. They've got this beautiful shell of sesame seeds, so BYO floss, and they come with a little plastic bag of za'atar that looks like a bag of drugs. What you do is you rip off pieces of your bagel and then jam it into the za'atar so that the fluffy innards pick it up as it enters your mouth. It's so good!

So how do we make a great thing better? Stick a wiener in it. A hot dog, a sausage, a veggie dog even.

The best part about these is that you can make them in the oven *or* over a fire, similar to what I did almost every weekend in high school my junior year. "Wiener roasts," we called them, and we worshipped Costco hot dogs and the brand spankin' new website, Facebook, where we posted photos of our roasts. All you need are some long wooden dowels, available at Home Depot or Lowe's, and as many inappropriate wiener jokes as possible.

2 cups bread flour, plus more for dusting

1¼ teaspoons active dry yeast

¾ teaspoon kosher salt

1 tablespoon sugar

½ cup warm water

¼ cup warm milk

2 tablespoons olive oil

8 precooked hot dogs or sausages

Egg wash: 1 large egg yolk, beaten with 1 tablespoon water (only if using the oven method)

2 tablespoons toasted sesame seeds

2 tablespoons za'atar

Harissa ketchup (1 teaspoon or more harissa mixed with ¼ cup ketchup), for serving

In a large bowl or in a stand mixer fitted with a dough hook, stir together the flour, yeast, salt, and sugar. In a small bowl or measuring cup, combine the water, milk, and olive oil and then stir it into the flour mixture. Knead, either by hand on a lightly floured surface or with the stand mixer on medium speed, adding more flour if needed, until smooth, 7 to 10 minutes. Transfer the dough to an oiled bowl, cover it with plastic wrap or a damp kitchen towel, and let it rise until doubled in size, about 2 hours.

(recipe continues)

Oven method: Line a baking sheet with parchment paper. Divide the dough into 8 equal parts and keep it covered when you're not working with it. Working with one piece of dough at a time, roll out a long skinny snake and wrap it firmly and evenly around a hot dog. Roll it back and forth on your work surface a couple of times so that the coils of the dough stick together, and then place it on the baking sheet. Continue with the remaining dough and hot dogs, placing them 1½ inches apart on the baking sheet. Let them rise for 30 more minutes and preheat the oven to 350°F.

Brush the tops and sides evenly with the egg wash and then sprinkle liberally with sesame seeds and za'atar.

Bake until lightly browned. Begin checking for doneness at 18 minutes.

Let cool slightly and enjoy with lots of ketchup.

Campfire method: Start a bonfire! For each bagel dog, wrap a piece of foil around a long 1-inch-diameter wooden dowel so that it covers about 6 inches of length at the tip. Just the tip. Pinch off a plum-size piece of dough, roll it into a snake and wrap it firmly around the foil-covered part of the dowel. Roll it between your hands a few times to make sure there are no holes in the dough, and then stick it right above the fire. Rotate it so that it cooks evenly, and cook it gradually until it is browned evenly on all sides. (Make sure that it's not touching the fire at all, otherwise it will brown quickly on the outside but still be raw on the inside.) As you cook the bagel, stick a wiener on a pointy stick and warm it right alongside the bagel in the fire. Let the bagel cool briefly, then remove it from the dowel, using a paper towel to shield your hands in case it's still quite hot. The bagel should slip off pretty easily. If it doesn't, cook it a little bit longer.

Squirt the hole with ketchup and sprinkle in some za'atar and sesame seeds. Insert your wiener and enjoy!

McSORLEY'S CHEESE AND CRACKER PLATE

My friend Rob could make an empty cardboard box sound exciting. With the amount of thrill and persuasion that he injects into his voice when he wants to tell you about a cool new thing that he found, he could easily be one of the world's best salesmen. One day early on in my second year of college, he returned to the Juilliard dorms from an adventure downtown—this was before we discovered how fun going downtown instead of uptown was—with news of this bar that he had discovered, McSorley's Old Ale House. "It's so great!" He beamed. "You sit down in a sea of sawdust. And then you choose between two beers, light and dark, or you could get both, and then you eat crackers with raw onions and cheese and it's everything you've ever wanted while drinking beer. Grab Stoopie's ID, we're going this weekend!" On paper it wouldn't have sounded like much, but Rob was convincing, and besides, even pre-age 21 I was starting to feel the paralysis that all of New York's options gave me, so a bar with two beers and one token snack plate appealed to me.

It was empty when we walked in with our friends late after Sunday rehearsals, and as I kicked around the sawdust on the ground (better to soak up the blood and beer, apparently) it occurred to me that I'd been there before: 10 years prior with my dad, on my first-ever trip to New York. It was in broad daylight and probably wasn't even open, but we went in anyway and he had been so excited to finally take a peek into the bar where all of his friends went when he was at Juilliard. Only back then he wasn't allowed in because he had no older brother to get him a fake ID.

So I poured one out for my pop's college social life and then got to work on my two little beers. Rob ordered the cheese plate, passed it around, and he was right. A salty cracker topped with a crisp raw onion, sharp white cheddar, and *that strong-ass mustard* was everything that I wanted. Refreshing, nostril-clearing, crunchy, salty, and not too filling as to take away from my beer capacity.

"Let's make this a Sunday night tradition!" we agreed around the round wood table. We never returned. I don't know why.

Crackers: 1 sleeve of saltines

Cheese: cheddar, sliced on the thick-ish side (⅛ inch)

Onion: sliced raw white or yellow onion

Mustard: Coleman's mustard powder mixed with dark ale until it reaches your desired consistency

Serve on a plate, enjoy with beer.

BUTTERMILK-BATTERED FRIED GREEN TOMATOES

Makes 16

I spent a lot of time in Williamsburg, Brooklyn, for a little while during college with a tattoo-covered boyfriend who lived in a second-floor warehouse off the L train that was run on homemade kimchi and anarchist values. It was called the Hutch and was home to 10 or 12 vegetarians, an indoor greenhouse, and a surround-sound system that played Eyehategod and Mutant Supremacy into the small hours of the morning. It was the exact opposite of my Upper West Side classical music school existence and appropriate for the time I spent rebelling against the practice room in order to blog and try new food. Every Friday night the L train felt like Halloween, and the camaraderie built around quirky silent parties hosted in the back of parked U-Hauls in deep Bushwick felt kind of like camp.

We ate pickles in unmarked restaurants, dodged hummus fights on the outskirts of the build-your-own bike festival, Bike Kill, and bought all of our clothes from vintage stores; but perhaps my favorite takeaway from this chapter of my life was the fried green tomato at the now-closed Sel de Mer, on Graham Avenue.

It was a giant disk of chewy breadcrumb-coated batter with a thick slice of green tomato buried in the middle. It was so gloriously salty with just a hint of sweet and sour. I loved it for its high ratio of coating to tomato; it was almost like eating a savory donut. Here's a version that I make, inspired by that tomato. It's coated in a thick buttermilk batter that's not unlike a pancake batter and deep-fried and salted over and over to perfection.

Flavorless oil, for deep-frying

4 large green tomatoes, thickly sliced

Kosher salt

2 tablespoons cornstarch

1/4 teaspoon baking powder

1/4 teaspoon baking soda

Black pepper

1 1/4 cups flour

1 large egg

3/4 cup buttermilk

1 1/2 cups panko breadcrumbs

Yogurt or mayo, for serving

Pour 3 inches of oil into a large heavy-bottomed pot. Clip on a deep-fry thermometer and heat the oil over medium-high heat to 360°F.

Season both sides of the tomato slices with salt and set them aside.

In a medium bowl, whisk together the cornstarch, baking powder, baking soda, a few turns of black pepper, and ½ cup of the flour. Add the egg and buttermilk and whisk to combine. Place the remaining ¾ cup flour in a separate bowl. In another bowl, combine the panko with a pinch of salt and a few turns of pepper.

Coat the tomato slices in flour and then dip them in the batter, allowing any excess batter to drip off. Coat them in the panko and fry them in batches of 3 or 4 at a time for 3 to 5 minutes, until golden brown. Use a slotted spoon to transfer them to a paper towel. Season them with salt and serve with yogurt or mayo.

HUMMUS WITH MEAT ALL OVER IT

Makes 6 to 8 servings

Or, hummus and beef nachos.

Question: How do you make a plate of hummus filling enough for a bunch of big burly farmers?
Answer: Put meat all over it.

Question: What's appropriate party attire for your hummus with meat all over it?
Answer: Fresh parsley and pomegranate seeds.

Question: How do you convince a bunch of big burly farmers that it's okay to eat dainty pink pomegranate seeds?
Answer: More meat.

Question: What are some good spices that will flatter the meat that goes all over the hummus?
Answer: Cinnamon, cumin, and allspice.

Question: What are you making for your next party?
Answer: THIS.

2 tablespoons flavorless oil
1 large onion, finely chopped
Kosher salt
1 pound ground beef (85% lean)
1 teaspoon Aleppo pepper
2 teaspoons ground cinnamon
2½ teaspoons ground cumin
¼ teaspoon ground allspice

Black pepper
Hummus (page 20)
Tahini Sauce (page 23)
¼ cup toasted pine nuts
¼ cup pomegranate seeds
Zhoug (page 23)
Chopped fresh flat-leaf parsley, for garnish
Pita chips, for serving

In a large skillet, heat the oil over medium-high heat. Add the onion and a pinch of salt and cook, stirring, until soft and translucent, 5 to 7 minutes. Add the beef and sprinkle it with the Aleppo pepper, cinnamon, cumin, allspice, ¾ teaspoon salt, and a few turns of black pepper. Cook, breaking up the beef with a spoon or spatula, until it is fully cooked and no longer pink. Taste and adjust seasonings as desired.

Spread the hummus in a serving bowl and top it with the beef. Drizzle on the tahini sauce and sprinkle with the pine nuts, pomegranate seeds, and zhoug. Sprinkle with parsley. Serve with pita chips.

CRISPY OVEN FRIES
WITH FETA MUHAMMARA

Makes 4 to 6 servings

Cheese fries were the only food I can remember not ever being allowed to eat as a kid. Fruit roll-ups and gummy snacks, while blacklisted, occasionally wiggled their way into my school lunch by way of a Lunchable or some other glitch in the system; but cheese fries, not a chance. I would have bathed in a tub of that nacho cheese, despite the image of it clogging my arteries that my mom instilled in my brain.

After years of fantasizing about ice skating rink concession stand cheese fries and movie theater cheese fries, I realized that my parents weren't gonna tell me no to cheese fries on my birthday, so I started taking advantage of that and a tradition was born. Every year on May 22, no matter where I happen to be (ideally in close proximity to a Steak 'n Shake), I eat a pile of cheese fries and reflect on the year behind me.

This is a higher-brow version of my birthday cheese fries and it's one that you don't need to wait until your birthday to eat. It's made of oven fries that are actually salty and crispy enough to hold a candle to their deep-fried brothers, thanks to a nice cold ice bath that helps them withstand a longer baking period without burning. And it's topped with a feta-cheesy version of one of my all time favorite dips, *muhammara*, which is a Middle Eastern spread that's heavy on the roasted red peppers and nuts. It's a little bit sweet, a little bit spicy, and perfect on a bed of hot oven fries.

3 tablespoons kosher salt, plus more to taste

2 pounds russet potatoes, cut into wedges

3 tablespoons unsalted butter, melted

Black pepper

Muhammara (recipe follows)

Preheat the oven to 450°F. Line a baking sheet with parchment paper.

Stir 3 tablespoons salt into a large bowl of cold water until dissolved, then add a cup of ice cubes. Submerge the potato wedges and soak for 20 minutes. Drain the potatoes and pat them dry.

Toss the potatoes in the melted butter on the baking sheet and season with salt and pepper. Bake until browned, about 1 hour, tossing halfway through. Add additional salt and pepper if desired.

Top the fries with the muhammara and serve.

MUHAMMARA

Makes about 1¼ cups

1 large (8 ounces) roasted red pepper, homemade (see Note) or store-bought

¾ cup walnuts or almonds, toasted

1 clove garlic

¼ teaspoon crushed red pepper

½ teaspoon ground cumin

2 teaspoons lemon juice

2 tablespoons olive oil

1 tablespoon honey

2 ounces crumbled feta

Kosher salt and black pepper

In a food processor, combine the roasted pepper, nuts, garlic, crushed red pepper, cumin, lemon juice, olive oil, honey, feta, a pinch of salt, and a few turns of black pepper and blend until mostly smooth. (A few coarse bits of nuts and feta are okay.) Taste and adjust seasonings as desired.

Note: *To roast your own pepper, char in a 500°F oven, about 30 minutes. Let cool, peel, and remove the seeds and skin.*

ASIAN SCOTCH EGGS

Makes 4 eggs

I knew I loved Scotch eggs long before I even tasted one, when they were nothing but a character starring in my British snack dreams. There is objectively nothing not to love about a Scotch egg. It's eggie, meaty, and fried. Done. Get me seven.

These use the flavors of my family's potsticker recipe to coat an egg that has an intensely runny yolk. They are messy creatures to make and eat, but boy are they worth it. Have them with mustard and beer!

6 large eggs

1 pound ground chicken

2 teaspoons sugar

2 teaspoons soy sauce

2 teaspoons rice vinegar

Black pepper

1½ teaspoons ground ginger

2 scallions, finely chopped

½ cup flour

1 teaspoon kosher salt

1 cup panko breadcrumbs

Flavorless oil, for deep-frying

Hot Chinese mustard (optional), for serving

Bring a large pot of water to a boil. Carefully lower in 4 of the eggs and boil for 6 minutes (this is for a runny yolk; if you want it firmer, add a bit of time). While they're boiling, prepare a large ice bath. When the 6 minutes is up, immediately transfer the eggs to the bath.

In a large bowl, combine the chicken, sugar, soy sauce, rice vinegar, a few turns of pepper, 1 teaspoon of the ground ginger, and the scallions.

In three smaller bowls, set up your breading station: In the first bowl, combine the flour, 1/4 teaspoon of the ground ginger, 1/2 teaspoon of the salt, and a few turns of pepper. In the second, whip up the remaining 2 eggs with 1 tablespoon water. In the third bowl, combine the panko, remaining 1/2 teaspoon salt, remaining 1/4 teaspoon ginger, and a few turns of pepper.

Cut out four 7-inch squares of parchment paper. Working with wet hands, divide the chicken into 4 equal parts. Place each part on a square of parchment paper and flatten out into a circle, about 1/2 inch thick. Carefully peel the eggs, coat them in a little seasoned flour, and then wrap each in chicken. It helps if you fold up the parchment paper to help the chicken onto the egg.

Once each egg is fully encased in the meat, coat it in the flour, then egg, then panko. Place back on the parchment and hold in the fridge until the rest of the eggs are ready to go.

Pour 3 to 4 inches of oil into a large pot. Clip on a deep-fry thermometer and heat the oil over medium-high heat to 360°F. Working in two batches, fry the Scotch eggs until they're golden brown and cooked through, 5 to 6 minutes. Serve with Chinese mustard and enjoy!

FRIED CHEESY PICKLES

Makes 12 pickles

Just as some parents of little ones are required to check for monsters in the closet, my mom was required to check for pickles on my burgers. Despite always ordering a very plain cheeseburger, an itsy bitsy pickle occasionally managed to wiggle its way on there and terrify me. Like, spider on my face in the middle of the night terrifying. And no, I don't really know why.

Luckily I've since gotten over my fear and embraced the pickle and thrown parties in its honor, and not just because they were cool in Brooklyn (okay maybe that was exactly why). And it's a darn good thing I warmed up to pickles, because cheesy fried pickles at the Toasted Frog in downtown Grand Forks are the quintessential late-night food around here. Just like Steak 'n Shake was quintessential in Glenview, just like pizza was in New York.

When the Ladies of Grand Forks Brunch Club convenes during the week, it's not breakfast for dinner, it's gin and tonics and pickles wrapped in Havarti cheese and egg roll skins and fried and then dunked in Sriracha ranch. They're *so good*. The chewy egg roll skin is what makes them addictive, while the crunchy sour pickle inside kind of creates the illusion that you're being healthy by eating a vegetable.

12 dill pickle spears

12 slices Havarti cheese

12 egg roll wrappers

Flavorless oil, for deep-frying

Ranch dressing mixed with Sriracha to taste, for dipping

Drain your pickles and use a paper towel to pat off any excess moisture. Wrap each pickle in a slice of cheese and then wrap each in an egg roll skin. Seal it well, using a bit of water on the edges.

Pour 2 inches of oil into a large pot. Clip on a deep-fry thermometer and heat the oil over medium-high heat to 360°F.

Working in batches, fry the pickles until golden brown and crispy on all sides, 2 to 3 minutes. Transfer to a plate lined with a paper towel and let cool slightly. Slice in half crosswise and serve with Sriracha ranch.

BASIC CHALLAH

Makes 2 loaves

An old friend from camp once told me that you can tell if a challah recipe is good by looking at how much oil and sugar there is in it. The more of those things, the better. *Amen.*

Challah dough is my safety blanket dough. I use it for everything. Donuts, babka, monkey bread. Its sweet, moist nature makes it adaptable to just about any shape and filling.

4½ teaspoons (2 envelopes) active dry yeast

1½ cups warm water

1 teaspoon plus ¼ cup sugar

6½ cups flour, plus more for dusting (or sub in up to 2½ cups whole wheat flour)

2 teaspoons kosher salt

4 large eggs

⅔ cup flavorless oil

¼ cup additional sweetener: sugar, brown sugar, honey, or molasses

Egg wash: 1 large egg yolk beaten with 1 tablespoon water

¼ teaspoon flaky sea salt, for topping

In a medium bowl, combine the yeast, warm water, and 1 teaspoon of the sugar and give it a little stir. Let it sit for about 5 minutes, until it becomes foamy on top.

Meanwhile, in a large bowl or in a stand mixer fitted with the dough hook, mix together the flour, salt, and remaining ¼ cup sugar. In a medium bowl, whisk together the eggs, oil, and additional sweetener.

When the yeast is foamy, add it to the dry mixture immediately followed by the egg mixture and stir to combine. Knead, either by hand on a floured surface or with the dough hook until you have a smooth and slightly sticky dough, 7 to 10 minutes, adding more white flour as necessary (but resist any urge to add too much!).

Transfer the dough to an oiled bowl, cover it with plastic wrap or a damp kitchen towel, and let it sit at room temperature until it has doubled in size, about 2 hours. (It will take slightly longer if you're using whole wheat flour.) Alternatively, you can stick it in the refrigerator overnight and then let it sit at room temperature for about 1 hour before shaping.

To shape the dough in the traditional braided way, go on to the next step. For other ideas, see the opposite page.

Line two large baking sheets with parchment paper. Divide the dough in half and, working with half of the dough at a time (keeping the other half covered), pat the dough out into a long rectangle, roughly 3 inches by 12 inches (this doesn't need to be exact). From this, cut 3 long and skinny rectangles and roll them out a bit to get 3 long snakes. Pinch them together at one end and then braid the snakes and pinch them at the other end. Transfer the loaf to a baking sheet and repeat with the remaining half of the dough. Let them rise, covered, at room temperature for 30 minutes.

Preheat the oven to 375°F.

Brush the loaves with a thin even layer of egg wash and sprinkle with sea salt. Bake until the loaves are golden brown and have an internal temperature of 190°F. Begin checking for doneness at 28 minutes.

Let the loaves cool until they're jusssst cool enough that they won't burn your mouth, and then enjoy with lots of butter.

Enjoyable Ways to Harass a Batch of Challah Dough

DEEP FRY IT (see sufganiyot page 201)

STEAM IT IN LITTLE BUNS

LACE IT WITH CHOPPED SALAMI (after its first rising)

MAKE A KING CAKE fill it with praline, top it with powdered sugar glaze and a gallon of sprinkles

MAKE A BABKA (see page 181)

SCALLION PANCAKE IT (see page 186)

WAFFLE IT (see page 60)

PRETZEL IT dip the loaves in a baking soda or lye bath before baking

SEEDUCTION CHALLAH

Makes 2 large loaves or 4 medium loaves

Eggboy here! I have a challah story for you.

Before we all turned to Egg, my family was your typical country brood. We spent our summer days tending to sugar beet fields, mowing an aggressive patch of grass, and going to St. Cloud for baseball jamborees. My sister cleaned her bedroom a lot. But one winter with the beets plucked, and snow fallen, we packed our bags for New York City. The only country bumpkin to have ever before managed the journey warned simply: "Do not attract attention." So there we were, clad in black from hat to shoe, four sad looking Minnesotans. Upon our arrival, we were shocked to find ourselves the only people dressed in such a manner, and so quickly corrected our mistake with matching NY beanies, colored bright baby blue.

Our agenda passed us from Times Square (lunch at Sbarro), to the Empire State Building, and eventually, to Grand Central Station. Two things to know about the family futurely known as Egg: (1) Vacation is a code word for walking and (2) walking is a code word for eating superabundant servings of bread, which fueled the walking, which demanded more bread, and so forth. So on that day, in the recesses of Grand Central Station, you would have found us in a state of wide-eyed disbelief standing in front of the bakery kiosk staring at a gleaming, braided, handsomely browned loaf of the like we had never seen! "That one, that one!" we begged. Our parents needed no convincing. Hungry from our trek of the day, we surrendered civility and grabbed with pleasant aggression. Our mouths full, a muted voice called for more "pull-apart-bread." And so a name was born.

Years later, my Jewish, trumpet-toting, Long Island–born college roommate Mike caught me in our room. "Challah?" he said. I was confused. "Are you eating challah?" He repeated. I looked down at what little was left. "Pull-apart-bread." "Challah!" he exclaimed, excited, and impressed. "Where did you get that?" he asked, skeptically. "Grand Central Station, it's a family tradition," I told him, pleased with myself. It was a Lutheran, *Andy Griffith* fanatic from Minnesota schooling him on family ties to his ancient, sacred Jewish staple. He smiled wide, still in disbelief, and I pulled off a piece for him.

(recipe continues)

4½ teaspoons (2 envelopes)
active dry yeast

1½ cups warm water

1 teaspoon plus ¼ cup sugar

4 cups flour, plus more for dusting

2½ cups whole wheat flour

1 tablespoon kosher salt

½ cup pumpkin seeds, plus more
for topping

¼ cup sunflower seeds, plus more
for topping

¼ cup flaxseeds

¼ cup millet

2 tablespoons poppy seeds

2 tablespoons sesame seeds,
plus more for topping

4 large eggs

⅔ cup flavorless oil

¼ cup molasses or honey

Egg wash: 1 large egg yolk beaten with
1 tablespoon water

In a medium bowl, combine the yeast, warm water, and 1 teaspoon of the sugar and give it a little stir. Let it sit for about 5 minutes, until it becomes foamy on top.

Meanwhile, in a large bowl or in a stand mixer fitted with the dough hook, mix together the flours, salt, remaining ¼ cup sugar, pumpkin seeds, sunflower seeds, flaxseeds, millet, poppy seeds, and sesame seeds. In a medium bowl, whisk together the eggs, oil, and molasses or honey.

When the yeast is foamy, add it to the dry mixture immediately followed by the egg mixture and stir to combine. Knead, either by hand on a floured surface or with the dough hook until you have a nice smooth dough, 7 to 10 minutes, adding more white flour as necessary (but try not too add too much).

Transfer the dough to an oiled bowl, cover it with plastic wrap or a damp kitchen towel, and let it sit at room temperature until it has doubled in size, 2 to 3 hours. Alternatively, you can stick it in the refrigerator overnight and then let it sit at room temperature for about 1 hour before shaping.

To shape it in traditional braided loaves, refer to the shaping directions on page 177.

To shape it in a swirly shape: Line two baking sheets with parchment paper. Divide the dough in quarters and roll each out into long skinny logs, about 18 inches long, and then coil each one up like a snail. Place 2 loaves at least 3 inches apart on each baking sheet and let them rise, covered, at room temperature for 30 minutes.

Preheat the oven to 375°F.

Brush with egg wash and sprinkle with additional seeds. Bake until the loaves are brown and have an internal temperature of 190°F. Begin checking for doneness at 28 minutes.

PIMIENTO CHEESE BABKA

Makes 1 loaf

When I flew home for the holidays from New York, two Zabar's babkas were typically my ticket in the door, one for my mom, and one for our friend Marshy. The chocolaty crumbly coffee cakes packed like bricks in my suitcase and they withstood all the smooshing that happens in an airplane pretty darn well. Slowly over the course of my time home we'd pick at it and dunk it in our coffee.

Now whenever I visit New York, I always make it a point to visit Breads Bakery in Union Square, where the smell of fresh babka engulfs the place and hypnotizes me into buying way too many treats. Everything there is amazing, but their babka, made with layers of laminated dough and finished with a brush of syrup, glows from the shelf.

Here on the farm, I take a squishier savory approach to babka using my basic challah dough and filling it with the Southern staple, pimiento cheese. My knowledge of the South may be limited, but what I do know is that mayonnaise and cheese were a match made in guilty-pleasure heaven and it astounds me that it's not more popular in the Midwest. So rather than calling this a Pimiento Cheese Babka, it might attract more people at my parties if I called it Cheesy Swirly Bread; but then it'll all get eaten and there won't be any leftovers for me, so where is the fun in that?

Dough

½ recipe dough from Basic Challah (page 176), completed through first rising

Filling

¼ cup mayonnaise

¼ pound sharp cheddar cheese, shredded

1 jar (2 ounces) diced pimientos

¼ small onion, finely chopped

¼ teaspoon sweet paprika

⅛ teaspoon cayenne pepper

Kosher salt and black pepper

Egg wash: 1 large egg yolk beaten with 1 tablespoon water

(recipe continues)

Grease a 9 x 4- or 5-inch loaf pan. When the dough is finished rising, roll it out into a 10 x 14-inch rectangle. Spread on the mayo in an even layer, leaving a 1-inch border along one of the long edges. Sprinkle on the cheddar, pimientos, onion, paprika, cayenne, a good pinch of salt or two, and a few turns of black pepper. Starting at the long end opposite to where you left the border, roll up the dough to make a long jelly roll and pinch the edges to seal them shut. Use a serrated knife to cut the roll lengthwise down the center so that you have 2 long skinny pieces of dough. Position them so that the opening is facing up (so the filling doesn't all fall out) and then twist the two pieces around one another. Fold the dough in half, place it in the loaf pan, cover it, and let it rise for 30 minutes.

Preheat the oven to 375°F.

Brush the top of the dough with the egg wash. Bake until the top is golden brown and the loaf has an internal temperature of 190°F. Begin checking for doneness at 35 minutes. Cool in the pan for 10 minutes. Remove to a wire rack and enjoy.

ZA'ATAR MONKEY BREAD
WITH GARLIC AND ONION LABNEH

Makes 1 loaf

After the great Bundt cake incidents of 2012, 2013, 2014, etc., etc., the only way I'll go within 10 feet of a Bundt pan is if it's for monkey bread. This za'atar magic mountain is inspired by my friend Talia, who made it one Shabbat in Brooklyn for a large millennial food industry potluck. While chefs and entrepreneurs pulled out fancy seasonal citrus salads and A+ knife skills, Talia timidly opened up a tube of store-bought bread dough, dipped balls of it in butter and za'atar in a grandma-inspired move, and served it with a side of labneh and disclaimers.

It was one of the best dishes that night, though. What kept making us leave the deli resurgence arguments to get up for seconds and thirds were those fluffy herby balls that gave us the green equivalent of Cheetos fingers. They were almost like savory donut holes.

To recreate Talia's bread, I typically use challah dough (page 176), but you can absolutely use store-bought dough here. And a heaping pile of garlic and onions folded into its labneh accompaniment just might take you back to the oniony potato chip dip of your youth.

½ recipe dough from Basic Challah (page 176), made through the first rising

¼ cup unsalted butter, melted

¾ cup za'atar

1 cup labneh or plain full-fat Greek yogurt

4 cloves garlic, minced

1 small red onion, finely chopped

¼ teaspoon ground sumac (optional)

Kosher salt and black pepper

Olive oil, for drizzling

Preheat the oven to 375°F. Coat a 12-cup Bundt pan with cooking spray.

Divide the dough into 24 balls the size of golf balls. Dip them in the melted butter, roll in za'atar, and pile them into the pan. Cover and let rise for 30 minutes.

Bake until the bread reaches an internal temperature of 190°F. Begin checking for doneness at 30 minutes. Let cool for 10 minutes in the pan and then remove to the rack and cool slightly before serving.

In a medium bowl, combine the labneh, garlic, onion, sumac (if using), and a pinch of salt and a turn of pepper. Drizzle with olive oil and serve.

SCALLION PANCAKE CHALLAH

Makes 1 loaf

This is me in bread form! Chinese, Jewish, and pretty doughy, whether I can help it or not.

I originally developed this recipe for an article on a Jewish site where my assignment was to explain what it's like to be Chinese and Jewish. The answer is simple:

• Anything involving numbers and math comes really easily.

• You get to celebrate THREE new years.

• Family gatherings are all about eating carbs and no vegetables.

• Dating boys is RUL WEIRD*

Because one moment you're enjoying a first date with a boy who happens to be Jewish and the next moment he's planning the wedding because you mentioned you're Jewish and you're the first Jewish female he's met who doesn't remind him of his mother and suddenly it becomes clear that he has a very strong case of yellow fever.

That's basically it!

Bye!

½ recipe dough from Basic Challah (page 176), made through the first rising

1 tablespoon toasted sesame oil

3 scallions, minced

Kosher salt and black pepper

Crushed red pepper

Egg wash: 1 large egg yolk, beaten with 1 tablespoon water

Toasted sesame seeds

Preheat the oven to 375°F. Line a baking sheet with parchment paper.

Divide the dough into 3 equal parts and roll each part into a 12-inch log. Gently flatten each log so that it is about 3 inches wide. Brush each with sesame oil and sprinkle with scallions, salt, black pepper, and crushed red pepper. Roll the logs up lengthwise like a jelly roll and pinch the seams to seal. Lay the logs seam side down next to one another and pinch them together at one end. Then braid the logs and pinch them at the other end. Place the loaf on the lined baking sheet. Cover and let rise for 30 minutes.

Brush the loaf with the egg wash and sprinkle with sesame seeds and black pepper.

Bake until the loaf is golden brown and has an internal temperature of 190°F. Begin checking for doneness at 28 minutes. Let cool slightly and enjoy.

CHRISMUKKAH FOOD,
FEATURING THE ANNUAL DUMPLINGS OF THE WORLD PARTY

Growing up with Christmas and Hanukkah, I was truly #blessed. Celebrating the two gave the illusion of receiving double the Lisa Frank stationery and double the Keroppi pencil cases, and then on one weird year, I received the "larger combined" gift of an overhead projector. (It was, in fact, a crucial lighting element in our living-room dance recitals.)

Over the years, my family has gone through a rotating selection of holiday traditions, which have included everything from having afternoon tea at the Russian Tea Time followed by *The Nutcracker* at the Joffrey Ballet, to building gingerbread houses with pretzel sukkahs in their coconut yards. One of the silliest traditions though is our annual Dumplings of the World Party, where my mom sets up stations around the house with doughs, rolling pins, and fillings where guests can construct their own steamed buns, potstickers, samosas, and more. In our family cookbook there's an entire chapter devoted to dumplings, but each party usually has room for five, or maybe six different types. It's totally chaotic and we all just eat the dumplings throughout the night whenever they decide to be ready, and we never sit down for a formal meal. There's like a 50:1 ratio of dumplings to guests so everyone goes into a food coma toward the end and that's how we know it's time to turn on *The Santa Clause*. Following are some old favorites as well as some new twists on the classics.

cheese blintz   steamed bun   sufganiyah   potsticker

SAMOSA KNISHES

Makes 12 knishes

The closest Indian restaurant to Grand Forks is 1½ hours away, in Fargo. Oyoyoy, I miss Indian food so much and would absolutely submerge myself into a hot tub of tikka masala right now if you gave me one.

Luckily I've made enough samosas over the years at our parties that I have a grasp on making a pungent tasty filling, tinted with the pretty yellow color of turmeric. But while they're typically fried, for as long as I can remember we've baked our samosas, maybe to clear up space on the stove for steamed buns and the like.

Just for funsies, and because in addition to missing Indian food I also miss easy access to Yonah Schimmel, Queen of the Lower East Side Knishery, these are shaped into mini knishes and labeled as such.

Kosher salt

1½ pounds russet potatoes, cut into ½-inch cubes

3 tablespoons olive oil

1 medium onion, finely chopped

4 cloves garlic, minced

1 teaspoon garam masala

½ teaspoon ground coriander

½ teaspoon ground turmeric

¼ teaspoon ground ginger

¼ teaspoon sweet paprika

½ teaspoon cayenne pepper

Black pepper

½ cup peas, fresh or frozen

2 tablespoons lemon juice

14 to 15 ounces pie dough, store-bought or homemade

Egg wash: 1 large egg beaten with a splash of water

Yogurt and chutney, for serving

Fill a large pot with water, add 3 tablespoons salt, and bring to a boil over high heat. Add the potatoes and cook until tender, about 15 minutes. Drain.

In a large skillet, heat the oil over medium heat. Add the onion and a pinch of salt and cook until soft and translucent, 5 to 7 minutes. Add the garlic, garam masala, coriander, turmeric, ginger, paprika, cayenne, and a few turns of black pepper and cook, stirring, for 2 more minutes. Stir in the peas and potatoes and cook, stirring occasionally, for 15 minutes. Remove from the heat and stir in the lemon juice. Taste and adjust seasonings as desired.

Preheat the oven to 450°F. Line a large baking sheet with parchment paper.

Divide the pie dough into 12 portions, roll into balls, then roll each ball into a 4½- to 5-inch round. Place ¼ cup of the potato mixture in the center of each round and brush the edges with egg wash. Fold the edges up and pleat them, as if you were making a plump galette. Hug it between your hands a little so that everything sticks together and brush the outside of the dough with egg wash, too. Place them on the baking sheet 1 inch apart and bake until lightly browned, 20 to 30 minutes. Let cool slightly and serve with yogurt and chutney.

CHICKEN POTSTICKERS

Makes 24 potstickers

Since the day I could say *thoy thauthe*—that's "soy sauce" with a lisp—my favorite potstickers have been my mom's. Which is unusual since my dad's the Chinese one, but sometime early on in their marriage, my mom took a dim sum making class and came up with a recipe for these potstickers. There are two things I love most about them: their extra doughy wrappers, and the high concentration of fresh ginger. Rawr. So good.

It's not Chrismukkah without these potstickers, they're *always* at our festival.

Dough

2 cups flour, plus more for dusting

1½ teaspoons kosher salt

½ cup boiling water

½ cup cold water

Filling

1 pound ground chicken

¼ teaspoon kosher salt

Black pepper

2 teaspoons sugar

1 teaspoon grated fresh ginger

2 teaspoons soy sauce

2 teaspoons rice vinegar

2 scallions, minced

⅓ cup chicken broth

Dipping Sauce

¼ cup soy sauce

2 tablespoons rice vinegar

4 teaspoons toasted sesame oil

2 scallions, finely chopped

A pinch of crushed red pepper

Flavorless oil, for frying

To make the dough: In a large bowl, combine the flour and salt. Slowly pour in the boiling water while stirring, until you have a coarse meal mixture. Stir in the cold water to form a dough.

Knead the dough on a lightly floured surface until smooth and slightly sticky, about 10 minutes, adding more flour as necessary. Cover the dough with a damp kitchen towel and let sit for 20 minutes.

(recipe continues)

To make the filling: In a large bowl, combine the ground chicken, salt, a bunch of turns of pepper, the sugar, ginger, soy sauce, vinegar, scallions, and chicken broth.

To assemble the dumplings, divide the dough into 24 balls. Roll them out into 4-inch rounds, flouring the surface as needed. Place 1 tablespoon of the filling in the center of each round and fold in half to make a half-moon shape, pleating the edges to seal well.

Bring a large pot of water to a boil.

In a large skillet, heat a thin layer of oil over medium-high heat. Working in batches, add the dumplings to the boiling water and cook for 4 minutes (see Note). Remove them with a slotted spoon, allowing excess water to drip off, and transfer to the hot oil (be careful because this step can get spitty). Fry until the dumplings are browned and transfer to a plate lined with a paper towel. Let cool slightly and serve with the dipping sauce.

To make the dipping sauce: In a small bowl, combine the soy sauce, vinegar, sesame oil, scallions, and crushed red pepper.

Note: *You can steam the dumplings instead: Line a bamboo steamer with blanched cabbage and steam over boiling water until the filling is cooked through, 10 to 15 minutes.*

HONEY RICOTTA BLINTZES
WITH CARAMELIZED ONIONS

Makes 10 blintzes

We are big supporters of the movement to stretch the meaning of "dumpling." By definition, a dumpling includes a dough that's boiled, fried, or steamed, blah blah blah. In our family, as long as it's one food inside another food, you're golden. Arancini, for example, made a popular appearance in 2010, and soy chorizo baked empanadas have long been a favorite of the kosher/vegetarian crowd.

These blintzes actually began their life cycle as pierogi, an addition from Stoopie's husband's Polish family. I liked filling them with caramelized onions and ricotta with honey; and then, of course, we fried them in a bit of butter before setting them on the counter to be destroyed.

But in recent years I've found that this same flavor combination works so well with a blintz, as fluffy blintzes are used to being stuffed with sweet ricotta. Covering them in a pile of sweet caramelized onions take them to an astronomical level (light years beyond the flimsy soggy camp dining hall variety that I grew up with), and since blintzes are best when they're right out of the skillet, this recipe lends itself well to the casual eat-as-they're-ready format of our dumpling parties.

P.S.: This dish is equally at home on your dumpling party table and on your brunch party table.

Caramelized Onions
2 tablespoons unsalted butter

2 large onions, thinly sliced

Kosher salt and black pepper

Blintzes
1½ cups whole milk

2 large eggs

1¼ cups flour

½ teaspoon salt

Filling
4 ounces cream cheese, at room temperature

1 cup whole-milk ricotta cheese

1 tablespoon lemon juice

1 large egg

2 tablespoons honey

2 teaspoons chopped fresh rosemary

A pinch of kosher salt

Black pepper

About ¼ cup flavorless oil, for frying

(recipe continues)

To make the caramelized onions: In a large skillet, melt the butter over medium heat. Add the onions, a good pinch of salt, and a few turns of pepper. Cook, stirring occasionally, until deeply browned and caramelized, about 40 minutes.

To make the blintzes: In a blender or food processor, combine the milk, eggs, flour, and salt and blend until smooth. Let the mixture sit at room temperature for 30 minutes.

Coat a 9- or 10-inch nonstick skillet with a thin layer of oil, and heat over medium heat. Add ⅓ cup batter to the pan and tilt it so that it distributes evenly into a round. Cook until the top is set, the bottom is slightly browned, and it pulls away easily from the pan, 60 to 90 seconds. Use an offset spatula to transfer it to a plate or work surface (correct, you will not be flipping these). Repeat this process, stacking the cooked blintzes separated by sheets of parchment paper.

To make the filling: In a bowl, mix together the cream cheese, ricotta, lemon juice, egg, honey, rosemary, salt, and a few turns of pepper until combined.

To assemble: Place a blintz, browned side up, on a work surface. Spoon ¼ cup filling slightly below the center line of the blintz. Fold the bottom third of the blintz up over the filling and then fold in the sides. Bring the top third of the blintz down over the filling to seal. Set aside and repeat with the remaining blintzes.

In a large skillet, heat a thin layer of oil over medium-high heat until shimmering. Fry the blintzes a few at a time, until golden brown, 2 to 3 minutes on each side, adding additional oil if the pan dries out. Transfer to a serving plate, top with the caramelized onions, and enjoy.

A PAIR OF NICE BUNS

Makes 16 buns

Potstickers are a dumpling party staple, samosas are a dumpling party staple, but year after year, the award for popularity goes to the large fluffy buns that emerge ceremoniously from my mom's double-decker steamer. They are puffy balls of sweet wonderment that pull at the heartstrings of every kid who's ever fantasized about a world with no crust. They are the complete opposite of a crusty French baguette and within them lie such magical fillings as barbecued chicken or melted American cheese—or nothing at all.

American cheese was the first filling I remember my mom using for these, back when I pretty much only ate cheese and bread. And then the PB&J variation is an homage to the almighty Uncrustable, which doles out a similar heavenly sensation as eating these buns.

Note: If you want to go a more adult route and make a barbecued pork or red bean filling, I won't be mad! Feel free to use this dough and fill with whatever fillings you'd like. I'm also including shaping directions for making *gua bao*, or folded steamed buns (see Variation, below), which are nice if you want to fill your buns after they're steamed.

¾ cup warm water

¼ cup warm whole milk

2¼ teaspoons (1 envelope) active dry yeast

1 teaspoon plus ½ cup sugar

3 cups flour, plus more for dusting

½ teaspoon kosher salt

¼ cup unsalted butter, cubed, at room temperature

Fillings of choice (see Variations on page 200)

In a small bowl, swirl together the water, milk, yeast, and 1 teaspoon of the sugar and let it sit until it becomes foamy on top, about 5 minutes.

In a stand mixer fitted with the dough hook, mix together the flour, salt, and remaining ½ cup sugar. With the mixer running on low, pour in the yeast mixture and add the butter. Increase the speed to medium-high and knead for 5 minutes, adding additional flour if needed (just enough so that the dough doesn't stick to the bowl). Transfer the dough to an oiled bowl, turning to coat, cover the bowl with plastic wrap or a damp towel, and let it rise until doubled in size, about 2 hours.

(recipe continues)

Cut out sixteen 3-inch squares of parchment paper. Turn the dough onto a clean work surface and divide it into 16 balls. Keep the dough covered. Working with 1 ball at a time, flatten them into about 3-inch rounds, fill with desired filling, and pinch the edges shut to seal well and make a ball. Place each seam side down on a square of parchment paper. Cover and let rise for 30 minutes.

Bring a large pot of water to a boil over high heat and set a steamer over it. Place the buns in the steamer about 1 inch apart on their squares of parchment and steam until fluffy throughout, 15 to 20 minutes. Let cool slightly and serve.

American Cheese Buns

Fill each bun with a ¾-inch cube of American cheese.

This is like the softest ever grilled cheese. Okay, you don't have to use American cheese, you can use any cheese. But while we're on the subject of softer-than-Wonder-Bread buns, you might as well.

PB&J Buns

Fill each bun with 1 tablespoon peanut butter and 1 tablespoon jam.

Gua Bao (Taco-Shaped Buns)

To make steamed buns that you can be filled *after* they're steamed (see Schnitzel Bao, page 73), roll out the dough balls into ovals that are about 6 inches long and 3 inches wide. Brush them with a thin even layer of melted unsalted butter (you'll need 2 to 4 tablespoons melted butter total) and then fold them in half on the short edge. Proceed with a second rising and steaming as you would a filled bun.

ROSEMARY SUFGANIYOT WITH TOMATO JAM

Makes 12 donuts

Hanukkah donuts, or *sufganiyot*, were typically hacked when I was growing up by way of frying up disks of Pillsbury biscuit dough from the tube and then covering them with powdered sugar. With all of the craziness of the holidays and the dumplings that took priority, it was always nice to have such a reliable hack, and today it remains one of my favorite kitchen tricks, save for the one detail of having to withstand that terrifying moment when the tube of dough bursts open.

My other favorite donuts, however, are made from scratch and take a route that is closer to savory. There are enough sweets to pass around during the holidays, let the salt shine. I like filling my donuts with cheddar and dusting them with cheesy powder, but technically a *sufganiyah* is filled with jam or jelly, so here's a tomato jam sitch in a blob of fried rosemary challah.

2¼ teaspoons (1 envelope) active dry yeast

¾ cup warm water

1 teaspoon plus ⅓ cup sugar

3¼ cups flour, plus more for dusting

1 teaspoon kosher salt

1 tablespoon dried rosemary, finely ground

2 large eggs

⅓ cup flavorless oil, plus more for deep-frying

Flaky sea salt, for sprinkling

Tomato Jam (recipe follows)

In a medium bowl, combine the yeast, warm water, and 1 teaspoon of the sugar and give it a little stir. Let it sit for about 5 minutes, until it becomes foamy on top.

Meanwhile, in a large bowl or in a stand mixer fitted with the dough hook, mix together the flour, kosher salt, rosemary, and remaining ⅓ cup sugar. In a medium bowl, whisk together the eggs and oil.

When the yeast is foamy, add it to the dry mixture immediately followed by the egg mixture and stir to combine. Knead, either by hand on a floured surface or with the dough hook until you have a smooth and slightly sticky dough, 7 to 10 minutes, adding more flour as necessary (but try not too add too much).

(recipe continues)

Transfer the dough to an oiled bowl, cover it with plastic wrap, and let it sit at room temperature until it has doubled in size, about 2 hours.

On a lightly floured surface, roll out the dough to ½-inch thickness. Use a biscuit cutter to cut out 3-inch rounds, rolling the scraps until the dough is used up. Cover the rounds with plastic wrap and let rise for 30 more minutes.

Pour 2 inches of oil into a large heavy pot. Clip on a deep-fry thermometer and heat the oil over medium-high heat to 360°F.

Working in batches, fry the donuts for 1 to 1½ minutes on each side. Use a slotted spoon to transfer them to a wire rack. Sprinkle with flaky sea salt.

When the donuts are cool enough to handle, use a skinny knife to poke a hole in the sides and rotate it to create space for the jam. Use a piping bag to pipe the jam into the donuts and serve.

TOMATO JAM

Makes about 1 cup

2 pounds Roma (plum) tomatoes, cored and roughly chopped

½ cup sugar

1½ teaspoons dried rosemary

1 teaspoon kosher salt

A pinch of crushed red pepper

Black pepper

1 teaspoon lemon juice

In a saucepan, combine the tomatoes, sugar, rosemary, salt, crushed red pepper, and a few turns of black pepper. Set over medium heat and cook uncovered, stirring occasionally, until most of the liquid has cooked off, 1 to 1½ hours. Press through a fine-mesh sieve to remove the tomato skins and rosemary leaves. Stir in the lemon juice. Let cool and store in the refrigerator until ready to use.

LATKES

Makes 20 latkes

One Hanukkah, earlier than I can remember, Stoopie overdosed on latkes in a very real way, which resulted in us not having a fierce loyalty to them like other families. We had them occasionally, but Stoop typically fled the scene before I could even get out the sour cream. So we celebrated Hanukkah in other ways, with our menorahs that we painted at the paint-your-own-pottery place, and with piles of chocolate gelt, and Adam Sandler's "The Chanukah Song." And presents, obvs.

But during college I experienced a latke renaissance after tasting my ex-boyfriend's dad's rendition. They were thick like burger patties and guarded by a golden brown shell. I had never had anything like them. I could have overdosed right then and there.

Every year since then I've used a recipe inspired by that one, and I love putting out toppings beyond the traditional sour cream and applesauce to create a whole latke bar for all of my friends. (Never mind that I'm the only Jew at a party full of Scandinavians, they gobble them up.)

I like topping these with poached eggs and furikake, or mixing some scallions and kimchi into the batter and adding toasted sesame oil to the pan. The rule is that at least one latke during Hanukkah has to be downed with the classic sour cream and applesauce, but there are eight whole days of this holiday, so go wild with your latkes.

2½ pounds russet potatoes, peeled

2 medium yellow onions

1½ teaspoons kosher salt, plus more for sprinkling

4 large eggs

2 tablespoons lemon juice

Black pepper

⅔ cup flour

Flavorless oil, for frying

Sour cream and applesauce (or any other fun toppings), for serving

Using a food processor or mandoline, shred the potatoes and onions. Toss them with the salt and transfer to a cheesecloth. Use your hands to squeeze out as much liquid as possible.

In a large bowl, whisk together the eggs, lemon juice, and a few turns of black pepper and add the potato mixture. Stir to coat the potatoes evenly and then mix in the flour.

In a large skillet, heat ¼ inch of oil over medium-high heat, until shimmering. Use an ice cream scoop (and pack the mixture in firmly) to add portions of the mixture to the oil, spacing them out so as not to crowd the pan. Press the scoops down with a spatula to get ½-inch-thick patties. Fry until golden brown on both sides, for 2 to 4 minutes per side. Transfer to a wire rack or paper towel and sprinkle with salt. Repeat with the remaining mixture, adding more oil to the pan as needed. Serve with sour cream and applesauce, or any additional desired toppings.

A twice-fried latke is extra nice, so if you'd like to make these ahead of time, store them in the refrigerator and then reheat by frying them again.

LATKE SUNDAES WITH CHOCOLATE ICE CREAM AND CAYENNE SPRINKLES

Makes 10 servings

Obviously this is inspired by the deeply sacred act of dipping french fries in a Wendy's Frosty. So this latke's pretty basic and a logical thing to do, considering how well hot, salty, crunchy potatoes and cold chocolate ice cream go together . . . .

But wait there's more!

A few years ago, my friend Michelle from the blog *Hummingbird High* developed a recipe for homemade sprinkles and they blew my mind. They were essentially skinny lines of royal icing that were hardened and then chopped up, and they opened up worlds of possibility, like a chance to make any custom flavor I pleased.

So to this mix of hot, salty, cold, and chocolaty, I am adding spiiiiiicy by way of Cayenne Sprinkles. However, if you're short on time and don't want to fuss with a homemade sprinkle, top your sundae with a light dusting of cayenne and regular sprinkles.

Latkes (page 204), but omit the onions and add 1 more pound potatoes

2 pints chocolate ice cream

Cayenne Sprinkles (recipe follows)

For each sundae, top 2 latkes with a scoop of ice cream and cayenne sprinkles.

CAYENNE SPRINKLES

Makes about 1 ounce

1 large egg white

1¼ cups powdered sugar

½ teaspoon cayenne pepper

⅛ teaspoon kosher salt

Red food coloring (optional)

Line a baking sheet with parchment paper.

In a small bowl, whisk together the egg white, powdered sugar, cayenne, salt, and food coloring (if using). The consistency should be slightly thicker than Elmer's glue. Add a bit of water or more sugar if it is too thick or thin. Transfer to a piping bag fitted with a very small tip and pipe lines onto the parchment paper. Let dry at room temperature for 4 hours or overnight. Scrape the lines off of the paper and chop into sprinkles.

SWEET POTATO LEFSE
WITH ROSEMARY CREAM

Makes 20 lefse

Winter and lefse are required conversation topics for anyone new to the upper Midwest, apparently. Every time I met a new Egg or was introduced to one of their friends, the first thing they'd ask was "Have you survived a winter yet?" and the second thing they'd ask was if I'd tried lefse, the paper-thin holiday potato pancake from Norway.

I had winter covered from the beginning, with my bomber hat and dozens of new sweaters. Minus 15°F isn't actually that bad if you don't breathe the air directly. It was the lefse that was difficult. Not because it was an entirely new food that took months for me to understand, but because lefse—or more specifically, making lefse—is sacred. It's one of those things where everybody's grandma has a lefse recipe and everybody's lefse recipe is the best recipe, and when people make lefse, they *commit*.

It's not like flipping a latke where you could be leaning against the counter, drinking a beer with one hand, splattering oil all over with the other, and discussing the latest town gossip with your party guest, nope.

Making lefse, if it's not in your blood, takes time, practice, online tutorial videos, emergency trips to the store for a new skillet, frantic calls to your great-aunt-in-law Ethel, and a long wooden stick. Talk about a way to make a girl question whether or not she belongs in her new town. What I later learned was that lefse making should also include a team of people, not just your sad frustrated self. There should be someone to roll out the dough, someone to flip the dough, and someone to stand guard in front of the finished sheets with a butter knife and cinnamon sugar. The ladies in the local church groups have this down pat.

But what I'm afraid to tell the ladies in the local church groups is that I like my lefse made with sweet potatoes. Hugely untraditional, but I love the flavor and I love how it produces a beautiful, floppy sheet of orange pancake. To sweeten the deal, I like adding rosemary cream, because if you're gonna bastardize something, why not go all the way?

A typical lefse setup includes the following special equipment: a potato ricer, a pastry cloth, a ribbed rolling pin, a long skinny wooden lefse stick, a special lefse grill (which is large, flat, and very hot), and a jolly community of Norwegians who have been making lefse every year around the holidays for decades. Unless you live in Norway or the Midwest, some of these things might be difficult to find but that's okay. The bare

(recipe continues)

necessities are a potato ricer, a shallow skillet (ideally ½ inch deep or less), patience, a long skinny flipping apparatus such as an offset spatula, and a direct line to someone who knows what they're doing or some how-to videos cued up online. And flour! Tons of flour.

2½ pounds sweet potatoes, peeled and cut into 1-inch pieces

⅓ cup flavorless oil

¼ cup evaporated milk

¼ cup sugar

1 teaspoon kosher salt

2 cups flour, plus a whole lot more for dusting

Softened butter and sugar or Rosemary Cream (recipe follows), for serving

Bring a large pot of water to a boil over high heat. Add the sweet potatoes and cook until tender, 15 to 20 minutes. Drain.

Rice the sweet potatoes into a large bowl until you have 4 cups (there may be some left over, reserve it for another use). Add the oil, evaporated milk, sugar, and salt and refrigerate for a few hours until fully cooled.

Stir in the flour to make a dough. Divide the dough into 2 portions and roll each into a log. Cut the logs crosswise into 10 pieces each and keep them in the fridge as you work with one piece at a time.

Heat a shallow skillet over medium-high heat (or a lefse grill to 400°F). Roll out a piece of dough on a heavily floured work surface or pastry cloth until it is about as thin as you can make it, adding more flour as needed and flipping occasionally so it doesn't stick. Using a lefse stick or offset spatula, transfer the lefse to the pan (or grill) and cook for about 1 minute per side, until small brown spots appear. Transfer to a plate and cover with a clean kitchen towel to keep warm.

Continue making lefse, stacking them as they're finished. Spread with softened butter and sprinkle with sugar, or spread with rosemary cream and serve.

(recipe continues)

ROSEMARY CREAM

Makes about 2 cups

1¾ cups heavy cream

2 sprigs fresh rosemary

¼ cup sugar

2 tablespoons flour

A pinch of kosher salt

2 large egg yolks

In a saucepan, combine the heavy cream and rosemary sprigs and heat over low heat for 30 minutes, stirring often. Do not let it boil.

Meanwhile, in a medium bowl, whisk together the sugar, flour, and salt, then whisk in the egg yolks until combined.

Remove the rosemary sprigs from the heavy cream and discard. Measure out 1 cup of the heavy cream, cover it, and place it in the refrigerator to cool. Very gradually, pour 6 tablespoons hot heavy cream into the egg yolk mixture while whisking constantly (any remaining heavy cream can be discarded). Return it to the saucepan and heat over medium heat, continuing to whisk constantly, until the mixture thickens to a custard-like consistency. Pour the mixture into a heatproof container and cover it with plastic wrap pressed directly onto the surface. Refrigerate it for at least 1 hour, or overnight.

In a large bowl, beat the reserved 1 cup heavy cream to stiff peaks. Fold in the custard mixture.

SPECULOOS CAKE

Makes one 8-inch layer cake

Building a gingerbread house was a tradition that was alive and well in my life up until my first year on the farm when I spent all of my waking hours for a few weeks researching and building an almost-to-scale replica of the farm. It received the most extreme reactions out of the Eggs I've ever seen; Eggpop wouldn't let me throw it away after the holidays and is now hoarding it in his basement.

After my stint as gingerbread architect I decided that I should quit while I was ahead (or behind, depending on how you look at it), and I hung up my spatula. Gingerbread houses are fantastically fun to make and all, but don't you wanna eat it?? If it's good enough to eat, the walls are likely not sturdy enough, and you never want to fux with a less than sturdy wall unless you have cardboard and a hot-glue gun standing by to replace any broken walls. And emotional support.

So, here's one you can eat! It's a soft and moist cake that won't collapse as you're decorating it. It's flavored with a hefty plop of speculoos spread, like those gingerbread-y cookies you get on airplanes, so there's no need to get your whole spice rack out. But you SHOULD get your whole candy drawer out. Go wild with your decorations, buck wild.

Cake

1½ cups sugar

2¼ cups flour

1½ teaspoons baking powder

1½ teaspoons baking soda

1½ teaspoons kosher salt

2 large eggs

1 cup speculoos spread

1 cup buttermilk

¾ cup water

½ cup flavorless oil

1 tablespoon vanilla extract

Frosting

1 cup unsalted butter, at room temperature

½ cup speculoos spread

1 cup powdered sugar

⅛ teaspoon kosher salt

1 teaspoon vanilla extract

Candy and marzipan, for decorating

(recipe continues)

To make the cake: Preheat the oven to 350°F. Grease and line the bottoms of two 8-inch cake pans with parchment paper.

In a large bowl, whisk together the sugar, flour, baking powder, baking soda, and salt. In a medium bowl, whisk together the eggs, speculoos spread, buttermilk, water, oil, and vanilla. Add the wet ingredients to the dry ingredients and stir to combine.

Pour the batter into the cake pans and bake until a toothpick inserted into the center comes out clean. Begin checking for doneness at 28 minutes.

Let cool in the pans on a rack for 10 minutes and then remove to the rack to cool completely.

To make the frosting: In a stand mixer fitted with the paddle attachment, mix together the butter and speculoos until creamy. Gradually add the powdered sugar and mix to combine. Mix in the salt and vanilla.

To assemble the layer cake, level the layers and then stack them up with a thin layer of frosting in between. Use an offset spatula to frost the top and sides. Decorate with candy and marzipan to make it look like a gingerbread house or town.

IV

DESSERTS

CAKE

Decorating cakes is my favorite thing to do. I've never been able to draw or sculpt well, but with frosting, marzipan, and my large collection of cookie cutters, I feel like I can brute-force something into existence that would make my elementary school art teachers sorta proud. One of the first things that I learned when I worked at the town bakery was how to make clean straight edges with frosting and then how to pipe borders and the basket weave. It took time and patience, and when I Instagrammed my first decent-looking carrot cake, which had a scalloped border and carrots piped cleanly into the center of each slice, just as the bakers at the bakery taught me to do, my mom called me in a storm of worry that my cake was too basic and that I wasn't being creative enough.

So, when no one was looking, I experimented with different colors and frosting in the style of ombré. I dug around the bakery storage shelves and found edible shimmery dust and lumps of not-yet-expired marzipan, and when my sticky-bun-making duties were finished for the morning, I went to town frosting cakes and practicing my new spatula maneuvers. I began waiting for birthday orders to come in so that I could perfect my sprinkle skills and fine-tune my frosting penmanship.

When I stopped working at the bakery, I found every excuse to make a cake. I became the resident Eggfamily cake maker for birthdays, holidays, the #Eggwedding, and made-up occasions like grain-leg climbing parties.

My love of cakes isn't just about flexing my creativity. I like to think that when you eat a bite of cake or serve a slice to your afternoon guests or bail someone out of jail with a cake at hand that it's a highlight of your day—or at the very least not the worst part of your day. So if I can play any sort of role in making that happen on a regular basis, I'll forever be a happy human bean.

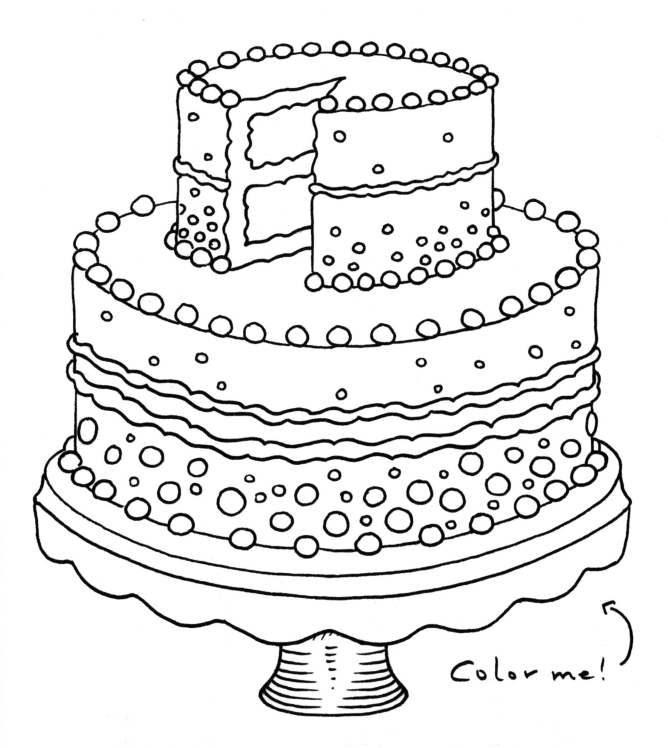

Color me!

MARZIPAN AND SEA SALT MANDEL BREAD

Makes 28 cookies

The reason I never loved mandel bread growing up is the reason I love it now: its dry, dense, crispy identity. It's the perfect edible gift to send to far-away friends due to its sturdiness and longer-than-most-cookies shelf life. Only my mandel bread crispness is disrupted throughout by the nice softness of marzipan rather than the traditional whole almond, so it's an enjoyable cookie on its own or dipped in whatever hot liquids you got in that mug.

7 to 8 ounces marzipan

1 tablespoon powdered sugar

3¼ cups flour

1 teaspoon baking powder

¾ teaspoon kosher salt

1 cup sugar

1 cup flavorless oil

3 large eggs

2 teaspoons vanilla extract

½ teaspoon almond extract

½ cup cacao nibs or dark chocolate chips

Flaky sea salt, for sprinkling

Pearl sugar or sprinkles, for sprinkling

Preheat the oven to 350°F.

Cut the marzipan into ½-inch pieces and toss with the powdered sugar. Set aside

In a medium bowl, whisk together the flour, baking powder, and salt.

In a large bowl, whisk together the sugar and oil until combined. Whisk in the eggs one at a time, and then whisk in the vanilla and almond extract. Use a wooden spoon to gradually mix in the flour mixture, marzipan, and cacao nibs or chocolate chips. (This dough can be made the night before and stored in the refrigerator until ready to use.)

Line a baking sheet with parchment paper. Divide the dough into 2 equal portions and place on the lined baking sheet. Mold the dough into two 14 x 3-inch rectangles about 3 inches apart. Sprinkle the tops with a few pinches of sea salt and pearl sugar or sprinkles.

Bake until the centers are set and the bottoms are lightly browned, 25 to 30 minutes. Remove from the oven and reduce the oven temperature to 250°F. Let the mandel bread cool slightly and then use a sharp serrated knife to cut crosswise into 1-inch-thick slices. Turn the slices on their sides and bake for 20 more minutes, or until desired crispness. Let cool slightly and enjoy with coffee, hot chocolate, or tea.

PISTACHIO LOAF CAKE

Makes 1 loaf

Despite my utter excitement at starting a new life in Grand Forks, I knew there would be some things that I missed about New York and that the transition wouldn't necessarily be as easy as a rhubarb pie. Sure, 95 percent of the time I enjoyed taking on the challenge of always making my own challah since it was impossible to get in town (and I suddenly had the time to), and using what unfancy ingredients I could find at the SuperTarget to make meals inspired by the fancy foods I had eaten in New York, almost as if that store was my *Chopped* box. But the other 5 percent of the time involved going red in the face and tweeting F-words when I couldn't find hazelnuts or I just. wanted. to. be. able. to. walk. out. my. door. and. buy. a. slice. of. BKLYN. Larder's. pistachio. cake.

Struggles! They could have been worse. But that fudgey nutty loaf cake! I neeeeeeded it badly and my cravings weren't ending. So I experimented and experimented and eventually came up with one that's similar and just as good. It took me a couple of years and some bulk bags of pistachios from the town Sam's Club. But I got it, you guys, I done got it.

1½ cups unsalted roasted pistachios

1 teaspoon kosher salt

½ cup flour; or ½ cup gluten-free flour with ¼ teaspoon xanthan gum

½ cup ground almonds

2 sticks (8 ounces) unsalted butter, at room temperature

1½ cups sugar

4 large eggs

Zest of ½ lemon

½ teaspoon almond extract

Glaze

1 tablespoon lemon juice

½ cup powdered sugar

Preheat the oven to 350°F. Grease a 9 x 4-inch loaf pan and line the bottom with parchment paper.

In a food processor, grind the pistachios to a fine crumb. Be careful not to overprocess or else you will end up with pistachio butter. Measure out 1½ cups of the mixture and transfer to a medium bowl. Set aside the remaining crumbs for the cake topping. Add the salt, flour, and ground almonds to the bowl with the ground pistachios and whisk to combine.

In a stand mixer fitted with the paddle attachment, cream together the butter and sugar for a few minutes until light and fluffy. Add the eggs one at a time, mixing well after each, then add the lemon zest and almond extract. With the mixer on low speed, add the dry ingredients and mix to combine. Scrape the batter into the pan and bake until browned on top and a toothpick inserted into the center comes out clean. Begin checking for doneness at 45 minutes. Let cool in the pan for 10 minutes and then turn out onto a wire rack to cool completely.

To make the glaze: In a small bowl, whisk together the lemon juice and powdered sugar and pour it over the cake. Top with the reserved ground pistachios and enjoy.

COFFEE HALVA

Makes one 6-inch wheel

To know me is to know that I'm probably going to name my firstborn Halva. If you've never had it, imagine a slightly softer, sesame-flavored innard of a Butterfinger bar, and then picture it on ice cream, folded into babka, smooshed between the layers of a cake, or devoured straight no chaser. It's nearly as versatile as a chocolate chip, and it's one of my all-time favorite things. This recipe is inspired by Michael Solomonov's method in *Zahav* and a piece of halva I had at the tiny Yom Tov Delicatessen in Tel Aviv, which contained layers of fine coffee grounds that broke up the sweetness of the candy and caused it to separate in layers, almost like a croissant.

Making halva is not something you should do if you're sleepy. Its steps are simple and easy to explain, but I need you to be *on* for this one. Have a bit of espresso, read all of these directions first, and be ahead of the beat when you're directed to add the sugar syrup, add the coffee grounds, turn off the mixer, and scrape it into the pan within the span of about 20 seconds. Mise-en-place the poop out of this, and you'll be on your way to halva glory in no time.

2 cups sugar

½ cup water

1 teaspoon vanilla extract

1½ cups tahini

¼ teaspoon salt

¼ cup very fine coffee grounds (grind in a spice grinder to the consistency of powdered sugar)

Line a 6-inch round cake pan (or a pan of similar size) with parchment paper, leaving 1-inch wings hanging over the sides.

In a small saucepan, combine the sugar, water, and vanilla. Clip on a candy thermometer. Heat over medium-high heat, stirring until the sugar dissolves. Once the sugar dissolves, stop stirring but continue to heat until the mixture reaches 245°F.

While the mixture is heating, in a stand mixer fitted with the paddle attachment, combine the tahini and salt. With the mixer running on low speed, carefully pour the hot sugar syrup into the bowl and stir just until combined. Immediately sprinkle in the coffee grounds and let the mixer go for 2 or 3 more revolutions just so that the grounds form a marbled effect. Quickly scrape the mixture into the pan. Use a spatula (or place a piece of parchment paper on top and use your hands) to press down on the halva to even it out as best you can. Allow it to harden at room temperature for 1 hour. Enjoy!

ITALIAN RAINBOW COOKIE SALAD

Makes 6 to 8 servings

The summer I moved to the Midwest was the summer that my perception of "salad" was turned upside down, held firmly by the ankles, and shaken free of all the vegetables that were hiding in his pockets.

It happened quickly and unexpectedly in a park outside of Fargo, and I held up the buffet line just slightly as I inspected a white glob of what I was told was salad. It came from a plastic bucket, it was white and fluffy, and what appeared to be chocolate bars peaked out at me like the curious small-town friends I hadn't yet made.

Cookie salad, I later discovered, is a Midwest specialty of crushed cookies and mandarin oranges, held together by Cool Whip and pudding and not an ounce of shame. No vegetables are required. And I sadly couldn't tell you what my first cookie salad tasted like, because I didn't eat it out of fear that I would like it and one day have to buy Cool Whip in public.

Part of me was relieved that my foray into vegetable-less salads began with a cookie salad and not the fabled Jell-O salad. But on the spectrum of Midwestern nonsalads, I had a long way to go before digging out Grandma's Jell-O molds. (Learning to pregame with a bowl of fresh spinach was just step one.)

As I pored over church cookbooks to learn the ins and outs of the beast, small triumphs came when it occurred to me that a cookie salad is not terribly different from an Eton Mess, and that its texture can be achieved with pastry cream and fresh whip, not boxed pudding and Cool Whip, and that despite the fact that it's called a salad, it's meant to be GOOD! Not misleading and bad. In the end, the largest triumph of them all came with the look on Eggboy's face when I told him to save room for dessert, *we're having cookie salad.*

This recipe highlights one of my all-time favorite cookies, the Italian rainbow cookie, which is actually more like a small three-layer almond cake. The cakey-ness of the cookies is what I love about this salad so much, because they sort of absorb the whipped cream and get even softer to almost create the illusion of eating cake and ice cream, but with more structural integrity since there's no melty ice cream to deal with. You can find these rainbow cookies all around New York, right next to the black and white cookies, but not much compares to the richness of a homemade one. This is perhaps the most labor-intensive cookie salad recipe in all of the Midwest. I won't be mad if you go the store-bought Italian rainbow cookie route or nix those cookies altogether and just stir leftover cake into this cream.

(recipe continues)

2 tablespoons flour

¼ cup sugar

¼ teaspoon kosher salt

2 large egg yolks

2 cups heavy cream

¼ teaspoon almond extract

4 mandarin oranges, divided into segments

¾ pound rainbow cookies, store-bought or homemade (about ½ recipe below)

In a medium saucepan, whisk together the flour, sugar, and salt. Whisk in the egg yolks and then whisk in 1 cup of the heavy cream. Heat the mixture over medium heat, whisking constantly, until it thickens to a pudding-like consistency. Stir in the almond extract, transfer the pastry cream to a bowl, and cover with plastic wrap, pressed up against the surface. Refrigerate for at least 1 hour or overnight.

Place the remaining 1 cup heavy cream in a large bowl or in a stand mixer fitted with a whisk attachment and beat until stiff peaks form.

Fold the whipped cream and chilled pastry cream together. Set aside a few mandarin segments and cookies for garnish. Gently fold the remaining mandarin segments and cookies into the cream mixture. Top with mandarin segments and cookies and serve.

ITALIAN RAINBOW COOKIES

Makes 32 cookies

3 large eggs, separated (see Note)

2 tablespoons plus ½ cup sugar

1 cup unsalted butter, at room temperature

6 ounces almond paste, chopped

½ teaspoon kosher salt

1½ teaspoons lemon juice

½ teaspoon almond extract

1⅓ cups flour

½ teaspoon green liquid food coloring

½ teaspoon red liquid food coloring

3 tablespoons apricot or raspberry jam

4 ounces dark chocolate

Preheat the oven to 350°F. Grease three 8 x 4-inch loaf pans and line them with parchment paper that comes at least 2 inches up the long sides of the pan. If you don't have 3 loaf pans, you can bake the layers in batches.

In a large bowl or in a stand mixer fitted with a whisk attachment, beat the egg whites to soft peaks. With the mixer running on medium, gradually add the 2 tablespoons sugar. Increase the speed to medium-high and beat to stiff peaks. Set them aside (see Note).

In a large bowl or in a stand mixer fitted with a paddle attachment, beat together the butter, almond paste, salt, and remaining 1/2 cup sugar on medium-high speed until light and fluffy, 2 to 3 minutes. Reduce the speed to medium and add the yolks, one at a time, beating well after each. Beat in the lemon juice and almond extract, then reduce the speed to medium-low and gradually add the flour. Mix to combine. Use a rubber spatula to fold in the whites.

Transfer one-third of the mixture to one of the loaf pans and use a small offset spatula to spread it out evenly. Transfer another third of the mixture to a separate bowl and fold in the green food coloring. Fold the red food coloring into the remaining third. Transfer these into the remaining 2 loaf pans, spreading them out evenly.

Bake until the tops are just set and no longer shiny. Begin checking for doneness at 12 minutes. Let cool in the pans for 5 minutes and then lift them out and place on a wire rack to cool completely.

Stack them up (from bottom to top: green, white, red) with 1 1/2 tablespoons jam between the layers. Wrap the loaf firmly in plastic wrap and refrigerate for at least 4 hours or overnight.

Melt the chocolate in a double boiler or by microwaving it in 30-second increments, stirring after each. Remove it from the heat and stir continuously until it is no longer hot. Spread it over the top and sides of the cookie loaf and stick it in the refrigerator to firm up for about 15 minutes. Cut into 1-inch squares and enjoy.

Note: With any recipe that calls for beating egg whites and then beating something else in the same mixer, I do a few steps to cut down on dishes and ensure that my egg whites don't have any bit of yolk in them, which will cause them not to beat to stiff peaks. I first separate an egg into 2 medium bowls. I then pour the white into my mixer bowl. Then I repeat for each egg, adding the whites one by one so that if one gets contaminated, they're not all ruined. And then I beat the whites to stiff peaks first, scoop them out of the mixer bowl, and then use the mixer bowl for the next step. If you use a rubber spatula to get 95 percent of the whites out, there's really no need to rinse the mixer bowl for the yolk step.

BROWN SUGAR COOKIES
(OR CHOCOLATE CHIP COOKIES
WITHOUT THE CHOCOLATE CHIPS)

Makes about 8 cookies

Years before I became hip to Levain or Birdbath (my two favorite cookie spots in New York), or Carol's Cookies (my favorite in Chicago), or the salty bittersweet chocolate chip cookie at the town bakery, Stoopie invented a cookie that is so jarring in principle it'll make you either scoot fast in the opposite direction or stick around just to see if the world explodes: Chocolate chip cookies without the chocolate chips.

!!

CHOCOLATE CHIP COOKIES WITHOUT THE CHOCOLATE CHIPS!
No, it's not just a sugar cookie, homogenous throughout and frosted with glee. It's a chewy, gooey, crackly puck that doesn't have a name to ride on or a trust fund under its butt. It's not decorated or fancy, all it has to offer is that it's a quality cookie.

These will show you that with all of the research put out into the world by Jacques Torres and J. Kenji López-Alt, one *can* achieve a beyond-terrific cookie sans the hook of them containing chocolate. Because a great chocolate chip cookie isn't great because it has chocolate, a great chocolate chip cookie is great because it has a foundation of gold, something we don't give enough credit to.

Is this getting preachy?

The point is, I appreciate the spaces filled between the chocolate chips, and just like I prefer my challah without any raisins, I often prefer my cookies without any chocolate to disrupt the perfect blend of butter and sugar.

3 cups flour	½ cup sugar
1 teaspoon kosher salt	1 cup packed dark brown sugar
1 teaspoon baking powder	2 large eggs
¼ teaspoon baking soda	1 tablespoon vanilla bean paste or extract
1 cup unsalted butter, at room temperature	Flaky sea salt, for topping

(recipe continues)

In a medium bowl, whisk together the flour, salt, baking powder, and baking soda. In a stand mixer fitted with the paddle attachment, cream together the butter and sugars on medium speed until pale and fluffy, 3 to 4 minutes. Add the eggs one at a time, beating well after each, and then add the vanilla. Reduce the speed to low and gradually add the dry ingredients. Increase the speed to medium and mix until the dry ingredients are incorporated.

Line a baking sheet with parchment paper. Scoop out hockey puck–size mounds of dough (about two ice cream scoops of dough balled up and flattened slightly) and place them on the baking sheet. It's okay for them to sit snugly up against each other for this step. Sprinkle the tops with a pinch of flaky salt. Cover with plastic wrap and refrigerate for at least 24 hours or up to 72. (In a pinch, you can bake these after just 1 hour of refrigerating, but curing the dough for 24 hours will yield the best results.) Feel free to bake these in batches or freeze some to bake at a later date (frozen cookies can be baked right out of the freezer, but they'll need more time in the oven).

Preheat the oven to 350°F. Line two baking sheets with parchment paper.

Place the cookies 3 inches apart on the baking sheets. Bake until the bottoms are lightly browned but the centers are still soft. Begin checking for doneness at 20 minutes. Cool on the pan on a rack for 10 minutes. Remove to the rack to cool completely.

CLOWN CONES

Makes 8 cones

Summer evenings in Glenview, Illinois, often included bike rides to the Baskin-Robbins, where I would march to the back of the store and retrieve my usual from the freezer: a creepy-ass upside-down mint chocolate chip ice cream cone decorated with bright frosting to look like a clown. As creepy as clowns are, I've just always had a thing for food decorated with faces, and the combination of mint chip ice cream and sugary buttercream frosting wowed my 6-year-old taste buds.

Here's a from-scratch version that you can make for your next circus party, *Clownhouse*-viewing party, or just anytime you feel like creeping out your friends. (No hard feelings if you'd rather make the proper adjustments for a narwhal cone or unicorn cone.) The ice cream here is inspired by the best fresh mint ice cream I ever had, from the Raw IceCream Company in New York. It is so creamy and fresh tasting, and it happens to be vegan. A small bit of vodka in the mixture makes scooping the ice cream easier; you won't taste the flavor of it though.

About 4 cups Fresh Mint Ice Cream (recipe follows)

8 cones, store-bought or homemade (recipe follows)

Colored frosting

M&Ms

Place a scoop of ice cream on a paper cupcake liner or a chocolate cookie (you can use the cookies from the Lindsay Lohan Cookies, page 92). Give it a cone hat and pipe frosting on for a face and hat decorations. Use small blobs of frosting to stick on M&Ms for the eyes and nose.

FRESH MINT ICE CREAM

Makes about 5 cups

1 can (13.5 ounces) full-fat coconut milk

¼ teaspoon kosher salt

½ teaspoon mint extract

1 teaspoon vanilla extract

2 tablespoons vodka

⅔ cup sugar

1 cup water

1½ cups raw cashews, soaked for at least 6 hours (or overnight) and drained

¼ cup firmly packed fresh mint leaves

4 ounces dark chocolate chips (optional)

(recipe continues)

In a high-speed blender, like a Vitamix, combine the coconut milk, salt, mint extract, vanilla, vodka, sugar, water, soaked cashews, and mint leaves and blend on high for 1 minute. Process in an ice cream maker according to the manufacturer's directions. Pour the mixture into a lidded container, fold in the chocolate chips (if using), place in the freezer, and freeze for 6 hours.

CONES

Makes 8 cones

½ cup sugar

½ cup flour

½ teaspoon kosher salt

A pinch of ground cardamom

2 large egg whites

½ teaspoon vanilla extract

¼ teaspoon almond extract

Preheat the oven to 375°F. Grease a baking sheet. Grease a 6-inch wooden cone mold.

In a medium bowl, whisk together the sugar, flour, salt, and cardamom. In a separate medium bowl, whisk together the egg whites, vanilla, and almond extract. Mix the dry ingredients into the wet mixture and mix until you have a smooth spreadable batter, slightly thicker than the consistency of glue. If it's too thick to spread, stir in some water, bit by bit, to thin it out.

Spread two 1½-tablespoon dollops of the batter into 4-inch rounds, at least 1 inch apart on the baking sheet. (Only bake 2 rounds at a time so that you have time to mold the cookies before they cool.)

Bake until the edges are lightly browned, 7 to 9 minutes. Working quickly (but carefully, so as not to burn your fingers), use a small offset spatula to flip a cookie over and then wrap it around a greased cone mold. Press the edges to seal it in place and then remove the mold. Stand it up with the pointy end on top, propping it up as needed, and cool fully.

Repeat with the remaining batter, greasing the pan and cone mold each time.

Psst··· *You can also use this recipe to make homemade fortune cookies! All you need to do is make 1-tablespoon 3-inch rounds instead and then fold them in half over a handwritten fortune and join the corners together. Let them dry in a muffin tin so their shapes hold.*

MUM'S SCHNAPPS BROWNIES

Makes 32 little brownies

File this recipe under "a relatively quick and easy thing to make in the event of a severe chocolate emergency." My mom started making these sometime when I was in high school and from the time they were cut into the squares until the time they were gone was usually no longer than a few hours. They're completely addicting, so it's probably very dangerous that they're so easy to make. I recommend setting up a game plan before you make these so that you have friends on call to come over and help you eat them once they're ready.

Brownies

½ cup flour

1 cup sugar

⅓ cup unsweetened cocoa powder

¼ teaspoon kosher salt

¼ teaspoon baking powder

½ cup unsalted butter, melted but not hot

2 large eggs

1 teaspoon vanilla extract

Glaze

1 cup powdered sugar

3 tablespoons unsalted butter, melted

3 tablespoons unsweetened cocoa powder

1 tablespoon peppermint schnapps

1 tablespoon honey

1 teaspoon vanilla extract

Crushed peppermints (optional), for topping

To make the brownies: Preheat the oven to 350°F. Grease an 8 x 8-inch baking dish and line with parchment paper, allowing 1-inch wings to hang over two of the edges.

In a large bowl, whisk together the flour, sugar, cocoa powder, salt, and baking powder. In a medium bowl, whisk together the melted butter, eggs, and vanilla. Pour the wet mixture into the dry mixture and stir to combine. Pour the mixture into the baking dish.

Bake for 25 minutes.

Meanwhile, to make the glaze: In a bowl, whisk together the powdered sugar, melted butter, cocoa powder, schnapps, honey, and vanilla.

When the brownies are finished baking, cool in the pan on a rack for 10 minutes. Lift them out of the pan and place on the rack. Pour on the glaze while the brownies are still warm and top with crushed peppermints, if desired. Let cool completely and then cut into 1 x 2-inch rectangles.

TAHINI BLONDIE ICE CREAM SANDWICHES

Makes 16 sandwiches

My favorite ice cream sandwich in New York was the brownie sandwich that came from the now-closed Bierkraft in Park Slope. The texture of the brownies was so similar to the texture of the firm ice cream, which was helpful in avoiding a situation of a too-hard cookie that smooshed all of the ice cream out the other end from where you bit it. They were almost like little ice cream cakes, and they were the perfect portable way to eat a brownie à la mode.

This rendition features vanilla ice cream swirled with tahini that's sandwiched between two tahini blondies, which are excellent treats in their own right and inspired by Danielle Oron, from the blog *I Will Not Eat Oysters*. If you'd like to sub the vanilla ice cream out for, say, pistachio or chocolate, I bet that'd be pretty darn tasty too.

1½ cups flour

¾ cup sugar

¾ cup packed light brown sugar

1 teaspoon ground cinnamon

¾ teaspoon kosher salt

½ teaspoon baking powder

¾ cup unsalted butter, melted but not hot

1¼ cups tahini

3 large eggs

2 teaspoons vanilla extract

2 pints vanilla ice cream

Sprinkles (optional), for serving

Preheat the oven to 350°F. Grease two 8 x 8-inch baking dishes and line them with parchment paper, allowing 1-inch wings to hang over all 4 edges.

In a large bowl, whisk together the flour, sugar, brown sugar, cinnamon, salt, and baking powder. In a medium bowl, whisk together the melted butter, ¾ cup of the tahini, the eggs, and vanilla. Add the wet ingredients to the dry ingredients and stir with a wooden spoon or spatula to combine. Divide the mixture between the two baking dishes and spread it out evenly with a spatula or your hands.

Bake until the center is just set. Begin checking for doneness at 23 minutes. Cool in the pans completely.

While the blondies cool, allow the ice cream to soften at room temperature to a spreadable consistency.

Using an offset spatula, spread the softened ice cream evenly over one of the blondies while it's still in the pan. Drizzle on the remaining ½ cup tahini and use the spatula to swirl it into the ice cream. Place the other blondie on top of the ice cream and freeze for 4 hours, until the ice cream is firm.

Using the parchment wings, lift the whole thing out of the pan and onto a cutting board. Use a sharp knife to trim the edges (if desired, this isn't necessary) and cut it into 1½- to 2-inch squares. Wrap individually in plastic wrap or place in an airtight container and store in the freezer. Dip in sprinkles right before serving, if desired.

PRINCESS CAKE

Makes one 8-inch cake

I fell in love with princess cake at first sight, which was probably after a plate of Swedish meatballs at IKEA. Almond cake, raspberry jam, and whipped cream in a house of marzipan. Cool, *I want a house of marzipan.*

I've read enough princess cake recipes to know that my version is not the most authentic version in the world because it's slightly simplified and doesn't involve the custard that sometimes wiggles its way in; but the almond cake within this boob is my oldest cake friend, my family's annual Valentine's Day cake.

It's the one recipe that I make every year at the exact same time, completely unchanged, save for its outfit. Here, it's decorated with marzipan circles made employing the technique that I used to make Sculpey clay beads when I was a kid.

Cake
¼ cup flour
½ teaspoon baking powder
3 large eggs, separated
¼ teaspoon kosher salt
¼ cup sugar
4 ounces almond paste, finely chopped
½ teaspoon vanilla extract
¼ teaspoon almond extract

Whipped Cream
¾ cup heavy cream
¼ cup powdered sugar
½ teaspoon almond extract

Assembly
¼ cup raspberry jam
14 ounces marzipan, kneaded with food coloring of choice if desired
Powdered sugar, for dusting

To make the cake: Preheat the oven to 350°F. Coat an 8-inch cake pan with cooking spray and line the bottom with a round of parchment paper.

In a small bowl, whisk together the flour and baking powder.

In a stand mixer fitted with the whisk attachment, beat the egg whites and salt to soft peaks. Then beat in the sugar, 1 tablespoon at a time. Continue beating to stiff peaks and set aside.

In a stand mixer fitted with the paddle attachment (you can reuse the egg white bowl without having to wash it if u lazy like me), combine the almond paste and egg yolks and beat on high for 2 to 3 minutes until pale and fluffy, scraping down the sides of the bowl as needed. Mix in the vanilla and almond extract.

(recipe continues)

Gently fold the whites into the yolk mixture, then fold in the flour mixture. Pour the batter into the pan and bake until a toothpick inserted into the center comes out clean. Begin checking for doneness at 30 minutes.

Cool in the pan for 10 minutes and then remove to the rack to cool completely.

To make the whipped cream: In a stand mixer fitted with the whisk attachment, beat the heavy cream, powdered sugar, and almond extract to stiff peaks.

To assemble the cake: Spread the jam all over the top and sides of the cake and then spread the whipped cream in a thick layer all over the top of the cake. Place it in the freezer while you prepare the marzipan (freezing the cake will make covering the whipped cream portion with marzipan easier).

On a piece of parchment paper or a surface dusted with powdered sugar, roll the marzipan out into a 12- to 13-inch round, dusting the top with additional powdered sugar if it's sticky. Gently lay the marzipan sheet over the cake and press down the edges at the base, trimming off excess marzipan.

CHOCOLATE AND VANILLA SLIDER CAKES

Makes 10 mini cakes

I am not the first to make a burger cake and I am not the last. And thank goodness, because holy moly are they cute! These little guys are as much about the process as they are about the finished product, and they're a miniature version of the classic big burger cake, so you can throw a mini cake party, have each of your friends make their own, and eat them like a real burger. Burger cake recipes come in all levels of difficulty, but here I've simplified it as much as I can, sticking to one basic cake recipe, a one-step "mustard" frosting, and simple marzipan details. It's still a good handful of steps, but it's intuitive and worth the oohs and ahs.

Cakes

1¾ cups sugar

1¾ cups flour

1½ teaspoons kosher salt

1½ teaspoons baking powder

1½ teaspoons baking soda

2 large eggs

1 cup buttermilk

1 tablespoon vanilla extract

½ cup flavorless oil

¾ cup water

⅓ cup unsweetened cocoa powder

5 ounces (¾ cup) dark or semisweet chocolate chips

2 tablespoons coconut oil

Fixins

12 ounces marzipan

Green liquid or gel food coloring

Powdered sugar, for dusting

Red liquid or gel food coloring

"Mustard" Frosting

1½ cups powdered sugar

6 tablespoons heavy cream

Yellow liquid or gel food coloring

Sesame seeds

To make the cakes: Preheat the oven to 350°F. Grease a half sheet (18 x 13-inch) pan and a quarter sheet (13 x 9-inch) pan and line the bottoms with parchment paper.

In a large bowl, whisk together the sugar, flour, salt, baking powder, and baking soda. In a medium bowl, whisk together the eggs, buttermilk, vanilla, oil, and water. Add the wet ingredients to the dry ingredients and mix to combine. Transfer 3½ cups of the batter to the half sheet pan and spread it out evenly. Sift the cocoa powder into the

(recipe continues)

remaining batter, stir to combine, and then pour it onto the quarter sheet pan and spread it out evenly. Bake the cakes until a toothpick inserted into the center comes out clean, about 15 minutes.

Let the cakes cool in their pans. Using a 2¾-inch round biscuit cutter, cut out 20 vanilla cake rounds and 10 chocolate cake rounds. (Note: covering the cakes and freezing them for an hour or overnight will make the edges of the circles cleaner, but this step isn't necessary.) Cake scraps can be reserved for making cake truffles, as snacks, or any other use you'd like.

Combine the chocolate chips and coconut oil in a microwaveable bowl and microwave in 30-second increments, stirring after each, until just melted and smooth. Place the chocolate cake rounds on a wire rack with a baking sheet or plate underneath to catch any excess chocolate and pour the melted chocolate over the cakes to coat the tops and sides. Place them in the refrigerator to allow the chocolate to firm up.

To make the fixins: For marzipan "lettuce," knead 4 ounces of the marzipan with a few drops of green food coloring (if the marzipan gets sticky, dust it with a little powdered sugar). Divide it into 10 equal parts and then flatten it out with a rolling pin or your palm to make flat rustic shapes that are slightly larger than the cakes.

For marzipan "tomato slices," knead the remaining 8 ounces marzipan with a few drops of red food coloring (if the marzipan gets sticky, dust it with a little powdered sugar). Roll it out to a ⅛- to ¼-inch thickness and cut out ten 2-inch rounds.

To make the "mustard" frosting: In a bowl, mix together the powdered sugar and heavy cream until smooth. Add a few drops of yellow food coloring. Transfer it to a piping bag fitted with a small plain tip or a zip-top bag with a small piece of a corner snipped off.

To assemble the cakes, stack them up in this order: a layer of vanilla cake, a squiggle of mustard, a layer of chocolate cake, lettuce, tomato, more mustard, another layer of vanilla cake, and a sprinkle of sesame seeds. Enjoy!

MOZARTKUGELN

Makes 12 kugeln

A cassette tape of my dad performing Mozart's clarinet concerto was playing in the hospital room when I was liberated from the womb, so Mozart has always held an extra special place in my heart. These days, enjoying a bit of Mozart means taking a big bite out of a Mozartkugel, one of my most favorite chocolates in all the land. Eggboy and I brought tons back from our honeymoon stop in Salzburg.

Mozartkugeln are layers of pistachio and almond marzipan filled with a chocolate hazelnut center and covered in a shell of chocolate. Their nutty chewiness gets me every time.

Hazelnut Filling

1½ tablespoons (about ½ ounce) dark chocolate chips

1 tablespoon heavy cream

3 tablespoons (about ½ ounce) finely ground toasted hazelnuts

Pistachio Marzipan

6 tablespoons pistachios, toasted

¼ cup powdered sugar

⅛ teaspoon almond extract

A pinch of kosher salt

1½ tablespoons light corn syrup

Almond Marzipan

¾ cup almond meal

6 tablespoons powdered sugar

¼ teaspoon almond extract

A pinch of kosher salt

3 tablespoons light corn syrup

Coating

6 ounces dark chocolate chips

To make the hazelnut filling: In a small microwaveable bowl, heat the chocolate chips and heavy cream for 30 seconds and then stir until smooth and homogeneous. Stir in the hazelnuts and freeze for 15 to 20 minutes, until firm.

To make the pistachio marzipan: In a food processor, blend the pistachios until they're very finely ground (but don't overblend or you'll end up with pistachio butter). Add the sugar, almond extract, and salt and pulse to combine. With the motor running, drizzle in the corn syrup and blend to form a dough. It may still look crumbly in the food processor, but if you squeeze it in your hand it should stick together. Pile it into a ball and wrap it in plastic wrap until ready to use.

To make the almond marzipan: In a food processor, combine the almond meal, sugar, almond extract, and salt and pulse to combine. With the motor running, drizzle in the corn syrup and blend to form a dough. It may still look crumbly in the food processor, but if you squeeze it in your hand it should stick together. Pile it into a ball and wrap it in plastic wrap until ready to use.

To assemble, divide both the almond marzipan and the pistachio marzipan into 12 equal portions. Keep the marzipan covered with plastic wrap when you're not working with it. Take one of the pistachio marzipan portions and smash it with your palm to make a flat round. Fold it over a rounded ¼ teaspoon of the hazelnut filling and roll it into a ball. Smash one of the almond marzipan portions with your palm and fold that over the pistachio ball. Roll it into a ball and place it on a plate or a parchment-lined baking sheet. Repeat with the remaining marzipan and filling and freeze the balls for 15 minutes.

To make the coating: Melt the dark chocolate either in a double boiler or in a microwave oven, heating for 30-second increments, stirring after each, until it is smooth and melted. Continue stirring until it is no longer hot to the touch.

One by one, dip the marzipan balls into the chocolate to fully coat. Allow excess chocolate to drip off and then place them back on the parchment. Harden them in the refrigerator or at room temperature.

MARZIPAN

Makes about 14 ounces

If my future firstborn's name is Halva, my second's will be Marzipan. Everything about it is perfect, even the trippy imagery it evokes from *The Nutcracker,* and it's my favorite decoration for cakes. It's like playing with Play-Doh in the best way possible. For marzipan that's strictly for a couple of minor cake decorations or for use as an ingredient within a big baked good, buying it from the store is a totally acceptable way to go. (See the notes on marzipan in the introduction, page xvii.) The reason I'm including this recipe here, however, is so you can have a respectable nut dough for when you want to reenact that page of *The Polar Express* when they're riding the train and eating little balls (of what I'll always believe to be marzipan), relive that time you stopped at the fancy soda place in Tel Aviv that served beautiful truffles of sugar-coated nigella marzipan, or want to give a gift of marzipan bars dunked in dark chocolate. Which is to say that this is the recipe you should make if marzipan is going to be the star of the show, either naked or covered in chocolate.

Marzipan is traditionally made out of blanched almonds, but making it with various types of nuts or seeds like pistachios, hazelnuts, or toasted sesame seeds is fun, too. Fattier nuts, like macadamias, require way less time in the food processor and way less (or even no) corn syrup to hold everything together. Macadamia marzipan in particular is less moldable, so I wouldn't recommend it for making shapes and decorations, but rolling it into balls and eating it straight is delish.

1½ cup nuts or sesame seeds (see headnote)

1 cup powdered sugar

1 teaspoon almond extract or other flavoring of choice

¼ teaspoon rosewater (optional)

¼ teaspoon kosher salt

6 tablespoons light corn syrup

In a food processor, blend the nuts until they're very finely ground and just starting to clump together (but don't over blend them or you'll end up with nut butter). Add the sugar, extract, rosewater (if using), and salt and pulse to combine. With the motor running, drizzle in the corn syrup and blend to form a dough. It may still look crumbly in the food processor, but if you squeeze it in your hand it should stick together. You may find that you don't use all of the corn syrup. Pile the marzipan into a ball and wrap it tightly in plastic wrap until ready to use. Store in the refrigerator.

HAWAIJ HOT CHOCOLATE

Makes 2 large or 4 small servings

Hawaij (huh-WHY-adge) is a Yemeni spice blend of which there are two very different types: hawaij for soup and hawaij for coffee. Hawaij for soup is heavy on the cumin and turmeric, while hawaij for coffee is more like what would happen if a squad of pumpkin spices went swimming in a pool of cardamom. As such, a tiny sprinkle in my morning coffee is enough to mask even the grossest of brews.

This hot chocolate is rich and creamy. Around the holidays, I like jarring up batches of the dry ingredients and tying them with a cute string and simple directions ("Whisk with a can of light coconut milk, add a splash of vanilla, heat, and enjoy!") and gifting them with a package of homemade marshmallows. It brings out the Martha Stewart in me, the Middle Eastern Martha Stewart.

1 can (13.5 ounces) light coconut milk

3 tablespoons sugar

¼ cup unsweetened cocoa powder

3 tablespoons tahini (optional)

1½ teaspoons Hawaij for Coffee (page 47)

½ teaspoon instant espresso powder

½ teaspoon vanilla extract

A pinch of kosher salt

Whipped cream, for serving

Rosewater Marshmallows (page 250), for serving

In a medium saucepan, whisk together the coconut milk, sugar, cocoa powder, tahini (if using), hawaij, espresso powder, vanilla, and salt. Heat over medium heat until warm. Serve with whipped cream and rosewater marshmallows.

ROSEWATER MARSHMALLOWS

Makes 16 large or 64 small marshmallows

Like wearing my favorite olive green handwash-only sweater, using rosewater makes me feel a little bit fancy without being too pretentious. It's a very easy way to elevate a plain-Jane vanilla marshmallow to something that's fit for a celebratory s'more or Hawaij Hot Chocolate (page 248). Or add a thick chocolate coating and give a batch as a gift.

¼ cup powdered sugar

¼ cup cornstarch

¾ cup water

¼ teaspoon almond extract

¾ teaspoon rosewater

1 teaspoon vanilla bean paste or vanilla extract

2 envelopes unflavored gelatin

¾ cup sugar

½ cup light corn syrup

⅛ teaspoon kosher salt

A few drops of red food coloring (optional)

In a small bowl, combine the powdered sugar and cornstarch. Coat an 8 x 8-inch or 9 x 9-inch baking dish with cooking spray and dust the bottom and sides with half of the powdered sugar mixture. Pour any excess mixture back into the bowl.

In a stand mixer fitted with the whisk attachment, combine ½ cup of the water, the almond extract, rosewater, vanilla, and red food coloring (if using). Sprinkle the gelatin over the liquid.

In a small saucepan, stir together the sugar, corn syrup, salt, and remaining ¼ cup water. Clip on a candy thermometer. Heat the mixture over medium-high heat until it reaches 240°F, then immediately remove it from the heat and bring it over to the mixer.

Turn the mixer on low and drizzle the corn syrup mixture in a slow and steady stream down the side of the bowl. Once the entire mixture is in, gradually increase the speed to high and let it mix for 7 to 10 minutes total, until lukewarm and fluffy. While the mixer is running, grease a rubber spatula and have that standing by the mixer, as well as the prepared pan.

Using your greased spatula, immediately scrape the mixture into your pan and spread it out evenly as best you can with the spatula. Dust the top with about half of the remaining powdered sugar mixture and then, if needed, you can use your hands to further flatten and even out the mixture. Let set for 1 hour. Cut into squares and dust the edges of the squares with the remaining powdered sugar mixture.

ROASTED RHUBARB MALABI

Makes 8 servings

Every spring a small patch of rhubarb appears in our backyard! It doesn't care that I've killed every herb I've ever tried to grow or that Eggboy is busy opening the fields for spring planting; it just kindly lets itself in, pours a glass of water, and plays with the cats until someone gets a hankering for a crisp or pie. The patch has been there for as long as anyone can remember, and I've become accustomed to making room in my freezer for a large bag of it to use throughout the year, like any good Minnesotan.

Here I've plopped it on top of a Middle Eastern milk pudding called *malabi,* which will always hold a special place in my heart since it's the dish that made me less weirded out by Jell-O salad, its very, very distant Midwestern cousin. A Jell-O salad consists of fruit or vegetables (or in extreme cases canned shrimp or ham) suspended in gelatinized juice or Mountain Dew or something of that sort. I had a lot of anger toward it during my first few months here because I didn't feel like meat Jell-O ever deserved the title of "salad." But I had an epiphany when I realized that if you just used coconut milk or milk as your base, flavored it with rosewater and vanilla, and stuck to toppings like fruit and nuts, you'd come wildly close to its couth Middle Eastern counterpart.

While you occasionally see malabi thickened with gelatin, I prefer using the more common cornstarch to give it a much creamier texture best presented in a glass rather than as a jiggly structure. (However, if you're genuinely hankering to use Grandma's Jell-O mold, then replace the cornstarch with 2 packets of unflavored gelatin, and keep in mind that it won't thicken on the stove, only when refrigerated.)

Crust

1 cup roasted pistachios

¼ cup sugar

A pinch of kosher salt

3 tablespoons coconut oil

Malabi

2 cans (13.5 ounces each) full-fat coconut milk

6 tablespoons cornstarch

1 tablespoon vanilla bean paste or extract

¾ teaspoon coconut extract

½ teaspoon rosewater (optional)

¼ teaspoon salt

½ cup sugar

Rhubarb

1½ pounds rhubarb, chopped into 1-inch pieces

¾ cup sugar

Zest of 1 lemon

1 tablespoon vanilla bean paste or extract

⅛ teaspoon salt

(recipe continues)

To make the crust: In a food processor, combine the pistachios, sugar, and salt, and blend to a coarse crumb. Add the coconut oil (it does not need to be melted) and pulse until the mixture crumbles together. Distribute the mixture between 8 serving glasses and use a muddler or the back of a spoon to press it down evenly and firmly. Set aside.

To make the malabi: In a medium bowl, whisk together ½ cup coconut milk with the cornstarch, vanilla bean paste or extract, coconut extract, and rosewater (if using).

In a medium saucepan, whisk together the remaining coconut milk, the salt, and sugar and heat over medium heat until simmering, whisking often. Pour in the cornstarch mixture in a slow, steady stream while whisking and then continue to heat while whisking until the mixture has thickened, 1 to 2 more minutes. Taste and adjust extracts and flavorings as desired. Divide the mixture into the 8 serving glasses (about ½ cup in each), cover, and chill for 4 hours or overnight.

To roast the rhubarb: Preheat the oven to 325°F. Spread the rhubarb on a rimmed baking sheet and top it with the sugar, lemon zest, vanilla bean paste or extract, and salt and cover with foil. Roast covered for 20 minutes, and then roast uncovered for another 15 minutes. Let cool. (Store overnight in an airtight container in the refrigerator if making this the day before.) Spoon on top of the malabi directly before serving.

CHOCOLATE HAZELNUT VEGAN HORSEY CAKE

Makes 1 horse (or one 8-inch round cake, if you haven't yet taken the horse pan leap)

The Dala horse is a common symbol in Scandinavian culture, so my obsession with my IKEA Dala horse cake pan is right at home in the upper Midwest.

Cake

1¼ cups flour or gluten-free flour

⅔ cup hazelnuts, toasted and finely ground

⅔ cup sugar

¾ teaspoon kosher salt

½ teaspoon baking powder

¼ teaspoon baking soda

⅓ cup coconut oil, melted but not hot

2 teaspoons vanilla extract

1 teaspoon lemon juice

¾ cup unsweetened almond milk, at room temperature

Ganache

4 ounces (about ⅔ cup) vegan chocolate chips

2 tablespoons coconut oil

1 tablespoon almond milk

2 tablespoons maple syrup, or to taste

Assembly

Crushed toasted hazelnuts

Sprinkles

To make the cake: Preheat the oven to 350°F. Grease a horse pan or 8-inch round cake pan and line the bottom with parchment.

In a large bowl, whisk together the flour, hazelnuts, sugar, salt, baking powder, and baking soda. In a medium bowl, whisk together the coconut oil, vanilla, lemon juice, and almond milk. Whisk the wet ingredients into the dry ingredients and then pour into the cake pan.

Bake until a toothpick inserted into the center comes out clean. Begin checking for doneness at 25 minutes. Let cool in the pan for 10 minutes and then turn onto a wire rack to cool completely.

To make the ganache: Place the chocolate chips and coconut oil in a microwaveable bowl and microwave in 30-second increments, stirring after each, until the chocolate is fully melted. Stir in the almond milk and maple syrup and continue stirring for a few minutes until the ganache cools slightly.

To assemble the cake: Spread the ganache over the cake so that it drips down the sides. Top with hazelnuts and sprinkles as desired. Enjoy!

CHOCOLATE CAKE WITH ROSEMARY BUTTERCREAM

Makes one 8-inch layer cake

Rosemary is my herb of choice, contrary to what my 21-year-old party-girl self would have told you. It was a focal point of my wedding bouquet, the name of my mom's mom, and in my opinion it's one of the prettiest, tastiest, and best-smelling herbs in all the land. I have oodles of jealousy for people who live in warm climates, where big healthy rosemary bushes line the sidewalks. Can you imagine a better way of spending your afternoon stroll than running your hands through fresh rosemary and then smelling them?

We have a big pot of rosemary in our dining room and Eggboy put him on a wheely scooter, so we kind of move him around as if he's a pet. But he's half-dead and would probably prefer some warmer weather.

Here's a classic chocolate cake that's got a little something *extra* in the form of a buttercream frosting that's been infused with rosemary. Infusing butter to make frosting is a *slightly* time consuming thing, but the concentration of flavor that moves into the butter is bright and present and wonderful. This makes a good birthday cake for that friend who is 29 going on 60. It's got the hipness of an infusion but the mature soul of rosemary.

Ooh! And here's a fun variation; for mint or basil frosting, sub out the rosemary sprigs for 8 fresh mint or basil leaves

Cake

1¾ cups sugar

1¾ cups flour

1 cup unsweetened cocoa powder

1½ teaspoons kosher salt

1½ teaspoons baking powder

1½ teaspoons baking soda

2 large eggs

1 cup buttermilk

1 tablespoon vanilla extract

½ cup flavorless oil

¾ cup boiling water

Frosting

1½ cups unsalted butter

4 sprigs fresh rosemary

2 cups powdered sugar

⅛ teaspoon kosher salt

1 teaspoon vanilla extract

2 tablespoons whole milk

(recipe continues)

To make the cake: Preheat the oven to 350°F. Grease and line the bottoms of two 8-inch cake pans with parchment paper.

In a large bowl, whisk together the sugar, flour, cocoa powder, salt, baking powder, and baking soda. In a medium bowl, whisk together the eggs, buttermilk, vanilla, and oil. Add the wet ingredients to the dry ingredients and stir to combine. Whisk in the boiling water.

Pour the batter into the cake pans and bake until a toothpick inserted into the center comes out clean. Begin checking for doneness at 28 minutes. Let cool in the pans for 10 minutes and then remove to a rack to cool completely.

To make the frosting: In a saucepan, melt the butter over medium heat. Add the rosemary, reduce the heat to medium-low, and cook for 15 minutes, stirring often. Strain out the rosemary sprigs and transfer the butter to a large metal bowl. Place the bowl in an ice bath and use an electric mixer to beat it until it becomes pale and fluffy, scraping the sides of the bowl as needed. Remove from the ice bath and beat in the powdered sugar, salt, vanilla, and milk. (Alternatively, you can make the rosemary infused butter ahead of time, place it covered in the fridge overnight, and then soften it slightly before beating it with the sugar, salt, vanilla, and milk.)

Level the cakes and frost as desired. To make an edible rosemary planter like the one pictured, crumble up the cooled cake and layer it in a large bowl with the frosting as if it were a trifle. Stick fresh rosemary sprigs in the top.

CHOCOLATE TAHINI CAKE WITH TAHINI FROSTING

Makes one 8-inch layer cake, one 13-inch by 9-inch sheet cake, or 24 mini cakes

Not many things in life are better than a rich, moist chocolate cake covered in buttercream and doled out with birthday songs and birthday wishes. But as my old timpani teacher used to say, "If it ain't broke, fix it anyway." Chocolate cake, meet tahini.

Chocolate cake and tahini go together fantastically, but not like bacon and eggs or peanut butter and jelly: They're not splitting the spotlight 50/50. Chocolate cake and tahini are more like my favorite ice dancing pair, Meryl Davis and Charlie White. Meryl is the cake, the star, the real-life Disney princess who has the power to make everything she touches turn to solid gold (see: *Dancing with the Stars* season 18). While Charlie's the tahini, the support, the knight in shining armor on his horse to meet his princess. Yeah, he's pretty freaking magnificent on his own, but tahini kind of needs to latch onto something in order for him to deserve a spot on the podium, like chickpeas to make hummus, or sugar to make halva, or an outstandingly terrific chocolate cake. So when the two come together and chocolate cake is able to shine her absolute brightest thanks to the strong support of a smooth nutty tahini, an X-factor happens that makes this pair one of the best in the world.

Someone once told me that they "don't like cake," but that they "love this cake." The tahini here sends an otherwise classic chocolate cake right over the edge into no-going-back territory.

Cake

1¾ cups sugar

1¾ cups flour

1 cup unsweetened cocoa powder

1½ teaspoons kosher salt

1½ teaspoons baking powder

1½ teaspoons baking soda

2 large eggs

1 cup whole milk

1 tablespoon vanilla extract

¼ cup flavorless oil

½ cup tahini

¾ cup boiling water

Frosting

1 cup unsalted butter, at room temperature

½ cup tahini

2 cups powdered sugar

⅛ teaspoon kosher salt

¼ teaspoon ground cinnamon

1½ teaspoons vanilla extract

(recipe continues)

To make the cake: Preheat the oven to 350°F. Grease and line the bottoms of two 8-inch cake pans or one 13 x 9-inch baking dish.

In a large bowl, whisk together the sugar, flour, cocoa powder, salt, baking powder, and baking soda. In a medium bowl, whisk together the eggs, milk, vanilla, oil, and tahini. Add the wet ingredients to the dry ingredients and stir to combine. Whisk in the boiling water.

Pour the batter into the cake pans or baking dish and bake until a toothpick inserted into the center comes out clean. Begin checking for doneness at 28 minutes for round cakes and 32 minutes for a sheet cake.

Let cool in the pans or dish for 10 minutes and then remove to a rack to cool completely.

To make the frosting: In a stand mixer fitted with the paddle attachment, mix together the butter and tahini until creamy. Gradually add the powdered sugar and mix to combine. Mix in the salt, cinnamon, and vanilla.

For a layer cake, level the round cakes and stack them with a layer of frosting between them. Frost the top and sides of the cake.

For a sheet cake, spread the frosting on top and cut into squares, or chill in the refrigerator until the frosting is firm and use a biscuit cutter to cut into mini cakes.

CARDAMOM CUPCAKES
WITH LINGONBERRY FILLING
AND CREAM CHEESE FROSTING

Makes 24 cupcakes

One of my top ten favorite things that I love about being married to a Norwegian person is the right to use cardamom whenever I please. Okay, I always had the right to use cardamom whenever I pleased, but I feel more ownership over it now, like I'm going to win more points with the Eggparents the more I use it.

I love cardamom's floral, woodsy, spicy qualities. Just a teensy bit goes a very long way. Here, it's added to my vanilla cupcakes, and complemented with lingonberry jam and cream cheese frosting, so at its core it's quite a simple cupcake, but it has that little extra sumthin sumthin that elevates it.

Cupcakes

2 cups sugar

2¼ cups flour

1½ teaspoons kosher salt

1½ teaspoons baking powder

1½ teaspoons baking soda

1 teaspoon ground cardamom

2 large eggs

1 cup buttermilk

1 tablespoon vanilla extract

½ cup flavorless oil

¾ cup water

Frosting

½ cup unsalted butter, at room temperature

8 ounces cream cheese, at room temperature

2½ cups powdered sugar

1 tablespoon vanilla extract

½ teaspoon almond extract

¼ teaspoon kosher salt

Filling

About ½ cup lingonberry jam

To make the cupcakes: Preheat the oven to 350°F. Line 24 cups of two muffin tins.

In a large bowl, whisk together the sugar, flour, salt, baking powder, baking soda, and cardamom. In a medium bowl, whisk together the eggs, buttermilk, vanilla, oil, and water. Add the wet ingredients to the dry ingredients and stir to combine.

Pour the batter into the muffin cups and bake until a toothpick inserted into the center comes out clean. Begin checking for doneness at 18 minutes.

Let cool in the pans for 10 minutes and then turn onto a wire rack to cool completely.

To make the frosting: In a standing mixer fitted with a paddle attachment, beat the butter and cream cheese until smooth and gradually beat in the powdered sugar. Add the vanilla, almond extract, and salt and beat to combine.

Using an apple corer, extract the centers of the cupcakes (stopping short of the bottoms), to create a little hole for the jam. Fill a piping bag with the jam and pipe a small blob of jam into the little holes. Top with a hefty bit of frosting and enjoy.

PARTY-TRICK PEANUT BUTTER CAKE

Makes one 8-inch square cake

This cake is great because it is so rich and peanut buttery that it does not need to be frosted. Of course, I won't complain if you do frost it, but my point is, this puppy can be whipped out and ready to eat in very little time. It is idiotproof, hangoverproof, and can be made in even the most unequipped kitchens, for brunch dessert, lunch dessert, or dinner dessert. I'd encourage you to memorize this recipe and make it if ever you find yourself bored in a foreign kitchen or around people you want to impress in a short-ish amount of time. It's the tastiest with the least amount of effort. Top it with a plop of yogurt, whipped cream, berries, a dusting of powdered sugar, or nothing at all.

1 cup sugar	½ cup buttermilk
1 cup flour	¼ cup flavorless oil
¾ teaspoon kosher salt	6 tablespoons water
¾ teaspoon baking powder	½ cup creamy unsalted, unsweetened peanut butter
¾ teaspoon baking soda	
1 large egg	Powdered sugar, whipped cream or yogurt, and/or fresh berries, for serving
1 teaspoon vanilla extract	

Preheat the oven to 350°F. Grease an 8 x 8-inch baking dish and line the bottom with parchment.

In a large bowl, whisk together the sugar, flour, salt, baking powder, and baking soda. In a medium bowl or large measuring cup, whisk together the egg, vanilla, buttermilk, oil, water, and peanut butter. Add the wet ingredients to the dry ingredients and stir to combine. Pour into the baking dish.

Bake until a toothpick inserted into the center comes out clean. Begin checking for doneness at 30 minutes.

Cool in the pan for 10 minutes. Remove to a rack to cool completely, or serve while it's still warm. Serve plain or with desired toppings.

COCONUT CAKE

Makes one 8-inch cake

This is the coconuttiest coconut cake in all the land. It's got coconut in the form of extract, oil, milk, and a big snow pile of flakes. I like it because it's extra rich and moist, which makes it an appropriate one-layer cake, and its one layeredness means it's easier to frost and quicker to come together. Which is perfect for when you forget that it's someone's birthday until the last minute. (But if you want a two-layer cake, feel free to just double this recipe.)

Cake

1 cup sugar

¾ cup flour

½ cup cake flour

¾ teaspoon kosher salt

¾ teaspoon baking powder

¾ teaspoon baking soda

1 large egg

1 cup full-fat coconut milk

1 tablespoon lemon juice

1 teaspoon vanilla bean paste or vanilla extract

½ teaspoon coconut extract

¼ cup coconut oil, melted but not hot

Frosting

½ cup unsalted butter, at room temperature

1 cup powdered sugar

A pinch of kosher salt

½ teaspoon vanilla bean paste or vanilla extract

2 tablespoons full-fat coconut milk

Assembly

4 ounces unsweetened shredded or flaked coconut

Fresh berries, for garnish

To make the cake: Preheat the oven to 350°F. Grease and line the bottom of an 8-inch round cake pan.

In a large bowl, whisk together the sugar, flour, cake flour, salt, baking powder, and baking soda. In a medium bowl, whisk together the egg, coconut milk, lemon juice, vanilla, and coconut extract until combined. Whisk in the coconut oil. Add the wet ingredients to the dry ingredients and stir to combine. Pour the batter into the cake pan.

Bake until a toothpick inserted into the center comes out clean. Begin checking for doneness at 28 minutes.

Let cool in the pan for 10 minutes and then remove to a rack to cool completely.

To make the frosting: In a stand mixer fitted with the paddle attachment, beat the butter on medium until creamy. Reduce the speed to low and gradually add the powdered sugar and beat to combine. Beat in the salt, vanilla, and coconut milk.

To assemble the cake: Frost the cake all over and cover with the coconut. Decorate with berries as desired.

GINGER SNOW CONES

In my book a perfect day isn't complete without snowfall, so it helps that I live in a real-life snow globe. My relationship with snow has always been very strong, but it got even stronger when I moved here and learned that when it's cold enough throughout the winter and there are a million times fewer people walking around, gross, disgusting brown slush is almost nonexistent. In my line of work, snow also provides a variety of uses, including acting as a perfect light reflector and diffuser for photos and serving as an instant caramel hardener. And then one time I packed up a basket of Taiwanese shaved ice toppings and set up a picnic for the Eggs where we sat around in a circle, dumped red bean paste and condensed milk onto the snow, and ate it from the ground. It was totally goofy. (Thanks for humoring me, Eggs.)

I should acknowledge that not every place in the world is fit for eating snow, since it might have a sidewalk under it that's been peed on or covered in chewing gum. For these ginger snow cones, use your best judgment and only use freshly fallen clean snow, and then go to town creating tasty yellow snow.

Also! If you mix this syrup with fizzy water you get ginger ale!

½ pound fresh ginger, roughly chopped (it does not need to be peeled)

2 cups sugar

4 cups water

1 teaspoon lemon juice

Fresh clean snow

In a large pot, combine the ginger, sugar, and water and bring to a boil over high heat, stirring to dissolve the sugar. Reduce the heat to low and simmer uncovered for 1 hour. Let cool and strain through a sieve. Discard the ginger (or use it to make candied ginger). Stir in the lemon juice and transfer to a bottle. This makes about 2 cups ginger syrup.

Fill a cup (or paper cones, if you've got 'em!) with clean snow, drizzle on the ginger syrup, and enjoy!

FUNFETTI CAKE

Makes one 8-inch layer cake or 24 cupcakes

During my first summer on the farm, the thing that kept me awake at night was Funfetti Cake, when all of my preconceived notions of how to re-create the most iconic cake of my childhood were shattered through months and months of testing. It's a vanilla cake with rainbow sprinkles scattered about, so all you need to do is pick out your favorite vanilla cake recipe and then stir sprinkles into the batter, right? Wrong. There are rules to respect, flavors to maintain, and an even dispersal of sprinkles to achieve. Many things can go wrong with a homemade Funfetti Cake and I found all of them.

• **The flavor of Funfetti Cake isn't just vanilla. It's the nostalgic elixir of clear vanilla.** I was tipped off to this by my friend Marian after she took a class on Momofuku's birthday cake. McCormick brand clear imitation vanilla does just the trick, and I like enhancing it with a wee bit of almond extract. Say what you will about artificial flavors, but you didn't actually flip to the cake chapter to be healthy, did you?

• **Not just any sprinkle will do.** You want bright pops of color that will maintain their saturation throughout the baking process. Again, go with something artificial here. I tested naturally colored sprinkles, naturally colored nonpareils, naturally colored homemade sprinkles, artificial sprinkles, artificial nonpareils, artificial sanding sugar, artificial homemade sprinkles, chopped colored marzipan, and a collection of found objects that included bachelor button petals, dried fruits, chopped mint, and black sesame seeds. The very clear winner each and every time was the artificially dyed cylinders that you can get from any grocery store, in the baking section or ice cream topping section.

• **The cake must be white, not yellow, like a typical vanilla cake.** And therefore should not contain egg yolks. This will cause the layers to pull in from the sides and sink just slightly, but that is an okay sacrifice.

• **It should be light and fluffy, *almost* sandy, but still moist.** Hence the cornstarch.

• **The sprinkles must be distributed evenly and then stay that way throughout the baking process.** The all-oil cakes that I was used to had batters that were just too thin to suspend the sprinkles midlayer.

(recipe continues)

I made layers and layers of cake that summer and cut into them to find sprinkles that had sunk to the bottom or textures that were slightly too squishy. I read every vanilla and white cake recipe that I could get my hands on and spent mornings at the bakery talking to Baker John about various ways to improve it. Finally, right before I just about threw in the spatula, I cut into a test cake, and there they were, all of the little sprinkles smiling brightly against a snow white background, floating with even spaces between them as if they had been placed there individually by the Pillsbury Doughboy himself. It's always in the last place you look, right? My new friends loved it, I made one for our wedding, and on the Internet, people were re-creating it! It made me so happy.

Eggpop believes that your days are defined by what keeps you up at night. In Glenview, Illinois, in 1993 it was Mufasa from *The Lion King* poster above my bed. In Manhattan in 2007 it was the parties way uptown, and 4 years later in Brooklyn it was glaring lights from the city streets below me and the dread of next morning's commute. Here on the farm, when my chickens are tucked in, and the tractors are cooled down, the silence gives way to being kept awake by a sprinkle-speckled, vanilla-frosted cake, and well, I'm down with that.

Cake

2½ cups flour

¼ cup cornstarch

1 teaspoon kosher salt

2 teaspoons baking powder

1 cup unsalted butter, at room temperature

1½ cups sugar

4 large egg whites

¼ cup flavorless oil

1 tablespoon clear imitation vanilla (I prefer McCormick brand)

½ teaspoon almond extract

¾ cup whole milk

½ cup rainbow sprinkles (artificially colored cylinders, not nonpareils, sanding sugar, or anything naturally colored)

Frosting

1¾ cups unsalted butter, at room temperature

3½ cups powdered sugar

⅛ teaspoon kosher salt

1½ teaspoons clear imitation vanilla

¼ teaspoon almond extract

2 tablespoons whole milk

To make the cake: Preheat the oven to 350°F. Grease and line the bottoms of three 8-inch cake pans or line 24 cups of two muffin tins.

In a medium bowl, whisk together the flour, cornstarch, salt, and baking powder.

In a stand mixer fitted with the paddle attachment, cream together the butter and sugar until light and fluffy, 3 to 4 minutes. Add the egg whites, one at a time, mixing well after each addition. Add the oil and the extracts.

With the mixer running on low speed, add the dry mixture and the milk in two or three alternating batches and mix until just barely combined. Using a rubber spatula, gently fold in the sprinkles until they're evenly distributed. Distribute the batter among the cake pans or muffin cups, spreading it out evenly if using cake pans.

Bake until a toothpick inserted into the center comes out clean. Begin checking for doneness at 25 minutes for cakes and 20 minutes for cupcakes.

Let cool in the pans for 10 minutes and then turn onto a wire rack to cool completely.

To make the frosting: In a standing mixer fitted with a paddle attachment, beat the butter until smooth and gradually beat in the powdered sugar. Add the salt, extracts, and milk and beat to combine.

Frost the cake or cupcakes as desired and enjoy.

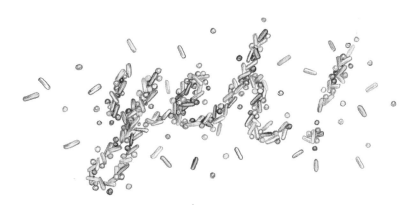

ACKNOWLEDGMENTS

This book is an extension of my blog, which brings me so much joy every day because of the love and support of its readers and fellow members of the blogging community. You consistently provide me feedback and encouragement and, overall, a sense of home in my little carved out corner of the internet. You are my family and this book would not have happened without you.

An immeasurable thank you to Jonah Straus, my agent, who guided me through this scary book birthing process with a patience and fierceness beyond what I ever could have imagined. And to the hard-working team at Rodale for believing in my vision for this book and bringing my story to life in wonderful, unexpected ways.

To Lisel Jane Ashlock, whose illustrations invoked utter shrieks of excitement every time I opened a new one. And to Chantell Lauren Quernemoen, whose magic eye brings out the joy and happiness in the people she photographs. I am so lucky to have been able to work with both of you ladies.

To Eggmom, for stepping in like a carrot-chopping, dish scrubbing angel from heaven when poop hit the fan in the shadow of my deadline. I will always be so massively grateful for this.

To Eggpop, for taste testing with clarity and helping to convert the farm into one giant photoset.

To those who helped test recipes, even when they were awful and "looked like cow pies": Cathryn Erbele, Jodi Regan, Tiffany Shiu, Lauren Cohn, Sarah Jampel, Danielle Larson, Sara Cornelius, Andie Taborsky, Stephanie Le, Sheila Liming, Dave Haeselin, Josh Scherer, Donny Tsang, Alana Kysar, Kristin Canham, Emily Montgomery, Joanna Keohane, my parents, Marshy, Stoop, Mia, Eggmom, and Nick.

To my assistants, past and present, for all the good work that they've done: Heather Schneider, Ellie Unkenholz, Lizz Denning, and Kristin Canham.

To the amazing companies who provided props, linens, and apparel for these photoshoots: Faribault Woolen Mill Co., Staub, Lodge Cast Iron, Stanley, Farmhouse Pottery, Canvas Home, West Elm, and Smeg.

To the chickens who provided the eggs for the recipes in this book: Macaroni, Macaroni, Macaroni, Macaroni, Macaroni, Macaroni, Macaroni, Macaroni, Macaroni, Macaroni, Macaroni, and last but not least, Macaroni.

To those far-away friends who regularly responded to my texts and pleas for book advice, ideas, and answers to bizarre questions with honesty, goodness, and weirdness: Mike Hedrick, Donny Tsang, Michelle Lopez, Alana Kysar, Stephanie Le, Josh Scherer, Jeff Gabel, Chris Thompson, and Lily Diamond.

To my friends and family who generously obliged when I asked them to come over for parties looking photo-ready and in "lumberjack-chic," "seasonless festive," and "cozy neutral" apparel. Thank you for never rolling your eyes at me in my presence and for being the greatest party guests in the world: Emily and Evan Montgomery, Mackenzie Teepen, Molly and Josie May, Tiffany Shiu, Kristin Canham, Eggsister, Eggparents, my mom, Marshy, Cathryn Erbele, Jodi Regan, Sheila Liming, Dave Haeselin, and Jason Sather.

To Sia for providing the round-the-clock soundtrack for writing this book.

To my dad, for having the wildest most fearless approach to foods that I've ever seen in a person, and for doing his best to pass this down to me. And also for his relentless support that did not waver when food and blogging took over more of my life than music.

To my mom, for single handedly teaching me the joy of cooking and baking, and for always being ready to test recipes and proof read. I found what I love to do because of her and she is my greatest inspiration in the kitchen.

To Nick, for inspiring me to work hard and encouraging me to be myself every single stinkin day. He tested these recipes, read and responded to every word in this book, and was my rock throughout this entire process. Not, like, a large garden rock that requires you to bend at the knees in order to lift, but a stonehenge rock that'd need a forklift or unknown supernatural methods to move. I love you, E-boy.

INDEX

"*Molly on the Range* strikes the perfect balance between quirk and comfort food: the sorts of spins on classics you'll want to use to make your friends think you're fun and cool. I'm sure she comes from a different planet, but everything is cute and funny and tasty there, and you're definitely invited; you just need a space suit. She's a relatable and endearing food-loving weirdo, and our plates are all the better for it."

—**MARIAN BULL,** writer, former editor of *Saveur* and *Food52*, tinyletter.com/messhall

"Molly Yeh's new book is a gem. Her stories (charming, funny, whimsical) make you want to befriend her, her recipes (clever, unfussy, tempting) beckon you to the kitchen, and when you finish reading it through (because this is one of those rare cookbooks you actually read), you wish there was more."

—**JANNA GUR,** author of *The Book of New Israeli Food* and *Jewish Soul Food*

"I've been a die-hard New Yorker for two decades. *Molly on the Range* makes me want to pack it all in and buy a farm down the road from hers so I can join the Ladies of Grand Forks Brunch Club, leave loaves of bread on each others' doorsteps, and share hotdishes. Her world is cozy, kind, and delicious on every level."

—**KAT KINSMAN,** senior food and drinks editor of *Extra Crispy*